Political Change

ELGAR DIALOGUES

Series Editor: *Frank Moulaert, Emeritus Professor of Spatial Planning, Department of Architecture, KU Leuven, Belgium*

This social science series engages in scientific dialogues on a wide spectrum of current issues. Scientific methodologies and conclusions, as well as public action experiences and recommendations, are discussed and presented.

The series aims to overcome the sterile state of scientific dialogue characterised by silo mentalities. It provides a proper stage for dialogical interactions and a forum for new and established voices to debate contending and contentious perspectives. It encourages scientists belonging to different traditions to enter into dialogue on epistemological stances, theoretical perspectives, research and action methodology. Such dialogues form a pertinent platform for building common ground in addressing the multifaceted challenges confronting society today.

Authors interested in submitting a proposal for the series are invited to contact the series editor Professor Frank Moulaert at frank.moulaert@kuleuven.be

Political Change through Social Innovation

A Debate

FRANK MOULAERT

Emeritus Professor of Spatial Planning, Department of Architecture, KU Leuven, Belgium

BOB JESSOP

Emeritus Professor of Sociology, Lancaster University, UK

ERIK SWYNGEDOUW

Professor of Geography, School of Environment, Education and Development, University of Manchester, UK

LIANA SIMMONS

Political Scientist, Food Activist, Italy

PIETER VAN DEN BROECK

Professor of Spatial Planning and Sustainable Development, KU Leuven, Belgium

ELGAR DIALOGUES

Cheltenham, UK • Northampton, MA, USA

Published by
Edward Elgar Publishing Limited
The Lypiatts
15 Lansdown Road
Cheltenham
Glos GL50 2JA
UK

Edward Elgar Publishing, Inc.
William Pratt House
9 Dewey Court
Northampton
Massachusetts 01060
USA

Paperback edition 2023

A catalogue record for this book
is available from the British Library

Library of Congress Control Number: 2022937624

This book is available electronically in the **Elgar**online
Geography, Planning and Tourism subject collection
http://dx.doi.org/10.4337/9781803925141

ISBN 978 1 80392 513 4 (Hardback)
ISBN 978 1 80392 514 1 (eBook)
ISBN 978 1 0353 2213 8 (Paperback)

Printed and bound by CPI Group (UK) Ltd, Croydon, CR0 4YY

Contents

Figures

Tables

Foreword

Olivier De Schutter

This volume provides an original and powerful contribution to an urgent debate: can social innovation bring about the democratization of the State rather than either leaving the socio-political organization of the State untouched, or being co-opted by the State apparatus? And if it can lead to such a democratization, how could this be achieved? Is there a form of social innovation that is best equipped to move beyond the dilemma of marginalization on the one hand and of cooptation on the other?

The consolidation of the State has been based, historically, on three powerful arguments. It relies, first, on an anthropological premise: individuals are selfish beings, motivated by the desire to expand their possessions and to pursue their life projects unimpeded by others. A powerful State is therefore necessary to avoid civil conflict, and substitute law and order to anarchy. Despite all their differences, this view is common to both Hobbes' *Leviathan* and Locke's *Second Treatise on Civil Government*. Second, it is said, the State is needed to create a framework conducive to the growth and flourishing of market relationships: its role is to enforce contracts, to unify measures, to create large markets (including in particular de-territorialized labour markets accompanying urbanization and the expansion of factories), and to protect property rights, and thus investment (Heilbroner 1985). Third, governance is about collecting information and planning development, and for this the centralization of power is essential: only the State, it is suggested, can gather the information needed to make the right choices in the name of general prosperity.

These arguments explain why the State has gradually become the main locus of power within society, so much so that "sovereignty" has been equated with the State itself—explaining in turn why concepts such as "food sovereignty" or "price sovereignty", referring to the establishment of relatively autonomous alternative food networks or of market relationships departing from the prices set anonymously by the market, are so powerfully subversive.

This genealogy of the State also has (at least) three consequences. The first and perhaps most significant consequence is that Capital and the State have since the start lived in symbiosis, in a process of co-evolution and mutual dependency. While capital depends on the State to accumulate, conversely, the State depends on such accumulation (and on economic growth more generally) to finance the services it provides to the population and thus to maintain its legitimacy. This is one major reason why the State is so inept at addressing issues such as environmental degradation or the persistence of inequalities and poverty—issues that, if they were to be addressed effectively, would require a restructuring of the market economy far more significant than what a "competitive" State could afford.

A second and related consequence is that social innovations that develop in the non-market sphere are bound either to remain marginal or to be captured by the State to avoid competing with the State's monopoly (or at least, centrality) in ensuring general prosperity. This, for instance, is one way to understand the conservatives' role in the birth of the Welfare State: in the years 1882–1889, the first social insurance laws under Bismarck's Germany were adopted both to undercut the attractiveness of communist ideas, which were perceived as a threat to the stability of the social order, and to marginalize mutual help societies established by workers' unions; and in the United Kingdom, the initial reluctance of unions to embrace State-led welfare essentially had to do with the desire to preserve the autonomy of cooperatives and union-led insurance schemes, especially at a time, in the early twentieth century, when universal suffrage was not yet established, and when the State was still perceived as chiefly aiming at the protection of the propertied class (Esping-Andersen 1990: 40; Gamble 2016).

The third consequence of this genealogy of the State was to lead to what Castoriadis calls the "privatization" of the individual (Castoriadis 1996:

25 and 77–79). Citizens are invited to vote at regular intervals to elect representatives who will then deliberate and decide on their behalf and, between two elections, they are expected to pursue their self-interest as economic agents on the market: they are asked neither to be creative nor to directly exercise power.

Against this background, the contemporary revival of the "commons" and the renewed emphasis on social innovations as a means to empower ordinary women and men to reimagine their environment can be interpreted as the result of three developments. First, the classic idea of the sovereign that emerged from the process of State formation between the fifteenth and the seventeenth centuries has lost much of its credibility. The past couple of decades have witnessed a "de-democratization" of the State, which has rendered this classic conception increasingly irrelevant and made it increasingly difficult for the governmental apparatus to regulate in the public interest. Such "de-democratization" has its source in the global trend towards devolution—the delegation of power to sub-national entities, regional or local. It also results from economic globalization—the lowering of barriers to trade and investment, facilitated by new technologies, by reduced costs of transport, and by free trade agreements and investment treaties. It is encouraged, finally, by the privatization of services and the rise of public–private partnerships. These trends work together, it has been argued, to create a situation in which the policymaking prerogative of States "has been redistributed 'up' to the supranational level, 'down' to lower State levels and 'across' to the markets" (Freeman 2017).

Moreover—and this is the second development—there are increasing challenges to the understandings of the individual, of the role of capital accumulation and of knowledge that, historically, have legitimized the dominant view of sovereignty. We are rediscovering that the individual is capable of cooperative behaviour and of altruism; that the restless pursuit of economic growth with the benevolent support of the State is neither environmentally nor socially sustainable; and that, in social transformation, "praxis" always precedes "theoria". In other words, the inventiveness and creativity of improvising social actors broadens political imagination beyond what we have come to expect from "experts", and the variety of local, context-based solutions exceeds whatever change can be imposed from "above" at the scale at which national governments operate.

Finally, the important role of social capital as an ingredient of sustainability leads to questioning the endless pursuit of the individualization of society produced by the current relationship between the State and the market. For those who dedicate their time and energy to launching and maintaining citizen-led initiatives, the building of social links is one of the most cited benefits expected from joining such initiatives (Seyfang 2009). Indeed, these are the source of "intrinsic motivations" amongst participants, who see value in investing in collective action quite apart from the question of whether the initiative shall contribute in any meaningful way to the professed end objective (such as building a circular economy, strengthening local resilience, or accelerating the shift to clean energy). It is in that sense that local-level, citizen-led initiatives may be seen as a "counter-movement", a reaction to the significant erosion of "social capital" in the 1980s and 1990s: the price paid for the process of individualization—resulting in a loss of trust and of social norms of reciprocity (Putnam 2000)—is now increasingly perceived as exorbitantly high.

Frank Moulaert, Bob Jessop and Erik Swyngedouw, with the support of Liana Simmons and Pieter Van den Broeck, ask the fundamental question of whether existing institutions can be transformed in order to adapt to these various developments. Is the State flexible and adaptive enough— are governments, from the local to the national level, flexible enough—to allow them to become allies of social transformation supported by social innovations? And if not, if they must be replaced instead, as argued by the municipalist approach of Murray Bookchin, then how should this be achieved?

Allowing ordinary people to co-construct solutions that follow neither the bureaucratic logic of public administration nor the profit-driven logic of markets requires what David Bollier and Silke Helfrich call "peer governance", a means of setting rules and enforcing them and of dealing with conflicts, in which "individuals see each other as peers with the equal potential to participate in a collective process, not as adversaries competing to seize control of a central apparatus of power" (Bollier and Helfrich 2019: 85). Peer governance, they write, is "distinct from governing *for* the people and from governing *with* the people [as in participatory modes of governance]. It is governing *through* the people" (Bollier and Helfrich

2019: 85). Classic modes of State administration, they explain, are incompatible with the spirit of "commoning" thus understood:

> To be effective and trusted, state power cannot just impose bureaucratic master plans; it must learn how to foster relationships among real people who have their own creative agency. This requires that we get away from the idea of human beings as units of need to which "service providers" must minister [...]. Focused on administering services, state agencies and service professionals tend to dismiss people's own creative talents, desire to contribute, and capacities for commoning. [They] neither recognize people's actual human agency nor strengthen that power. For their part, most people have internalized this image of themselves as passive consumers of professional and government services, and fail to regard themselves as potential participants in Peer Governance or the state polity. (Bollier and Helfrich 2019, p. 291)

Putting social innovation at the heart of public policymaking substitutes co-design for simple feedback as in New Public Management, or for consultation as in the more fashionable "multi-stakeholders" approaches. Ordinary people, the social actors, are neither "governed" nor are they "clients" whose needs must be catered to, nor even "participants" invited to feed into a policymaking process in which enlightened administrators or politicians have the final say. Instead, they are "agents", setting their own rules and governance mechanisms. And what is expected from the State apparatus is not simply to "respect" such self-governance, in the minimal sense of not imposing obstacles, but to "enable" it, by identifying the remaining obstacles and removing them one by one.

I welcome this important volume as a major contribution to this debate. The book combines three perspectives. These are based on a common diagnosis, yet they present a panoply of solutions. In that sense, the construction of the volume is coherent with the view of knowledge we now require. Solutions do not follow mechanically from an understanding of our predicament: they are to be invented, not discovered; and such invention can only be the product of our repeated attempts to experiment with new modes of setting up peer governance.

References

Bollier, D. and Helfrich, S. 2019. *Free, Fair and Alive: The Insurgent Power of the Commons.* British Columbia: New Society.

Castoriadis, C. 1996. *La montée de l'insignifiance: les carrefours du labyrinthe*, 4. Paris: Le Seuil.

Esping-Andersen, G. 1990. *The Three Worlds of Welfare Capitalism*. Princeton: Princeton University Press.

Freeman, D. 2017. *De-Democratisation and Rising Inequality: The Underlying Cause of a Worrying Trend*, Department of Anthropology and International Inequalities Institute, London School of Economics, Working Paper 12 (May).

Gamble, A. 2016. *Can the Welfare State Survive?* London: Polity.

Heilbroner, R. 1985. *The Nature and Logic of Capitalism*. New York and London: W.W. Norton.

Putnam, R.D. 2000. *Bowling Alone: The Collapse and Revival of American Community*. New York: Simon & Schuster.

Seyfang, G. 2009. Green shoots of sustainability: the 2009 UK Transition Movement Survey. University of East Anglia.

1   Can Mutual Aid in a Post-industrial Society Reforge the Political?

Frank Moulaert, Bob Jessop, Erik Swyngedouw and Liana Simmons

One of the big sources of disbelief in contemporary societal dynamics is that, despite thousands if not millions of socially innovative initiatives that have materialized across the world over the previous decades, virtually no democratizing political change is occurring. As if there were no need for it. Political dissatisfaction is stirring in the large majority of countries, nationalist and xenophobic populism is on the rise, 'law and order' political agendas receive growing support. At the same time, initiatives nurturing citizen participation, grassroots democracy or direct democracy, are blossoming. But the new grassroots 'political' experimentations only seldom converge with the socially innovative initiatives, even if these hold and experience significant innovations in socio-political mobilization and decision-making; and if such convergence comes about, its socio-political transformative impact rarely reaches beyond the local scale.

This book brings together three leading voices of contemporary social sciences to discuss and examine the factors of socially innovative initiatives and movements, their ambitions, their ambiguous attitudes towards and engagements with the political world, and their new ways of governing democratically. It also addresses the failures of contemporary democracies: their embeddedness in the global market, growing socio-economic inequality, impotence or refusal to engage in a democratizing discourse (such as equity narratives), let alone putting it into practice, and the lack of rootedness of politicians who are used to navigating the market for votes to connect to the material needs of large parts of the population. The book draws on a dialogical encounter between these three contemporary thinkers, which took the shape of a debate held at KU Leuven in 2019,[1] to explore socio-political agendas, strategies and movements seeking to overcome these failures.

This introduction is organized in five sections and focuses on the common ground, but also the missing convergence, between social innovation initiatives and movements on the one hand and the 'new' political on the other. Section 1.1 provides a brief history of the relationship between the development of community and polity from early society until now. Key in this analysis of the development of the relationship between social innovation and political movements is the rise and change in the societal role of civil society. Does civil society in its renewed role endow society with sufficient forces for the socio-political transformation that is badly needed? Section 1.2 examines some of the contemporary debates surrounding the relationships between social innovation, social change, political life and socio-political transformation today. It also provides definitions of key concepts used in the chapters that follow. Section 1.3 explains the three differing approaches taken by the three thinkers on the relationships between social innovation and socio-political transformation, as presented in the reflection chapters that follow (Chapters 2–5). Section 1.4 focuses on the points of tension emerging from the reflections, which form the framework for the dialogical encounter between the thinkers during the debate (Chapter 5), and which foreground suggestions presented for transforming the socio-political system by better reconnecting social and political concerns in society (Chapter 6). Section 1.5 concludes by providing an overview of the contents of each chapter in the book.

1.1   Community, polity and social innovation: a historical overview

At which stage did sociality, considered as essential for human life and community building, become (also) political? And at which moments in history did the social of the community drift away to become the politics of economic and bureaucratic elites? In this section, we analyse the historical evolution of the links between community, polity and social innovation, bringing to the fore the debate between mutual aid-based and market-oriented positionings in social innovation approaches. This debate reveals critical dimensions of the political and ideological natures of the social innovation debate.

To understand the historical evolution of the relationship between social relations and political life, we draw from authors who devoted a significant portion of their work to uncovering: how relations between humans have evolved (starting from early history); how sociality took on material and symbolic forms; how community was gradually built and disintegrated into more or less anonymous relationships between individuals and communities of shared practice (consumers, producers, labourers, …); and how this has affected political life and politics in the post-industrial society. In addition to our own work (Jessop 2015; Martinelli et al. 2013), we rely on the work of Karl Polanyi (2001 [1944]), Peter Kropotkin (1914 [1902]), Murray Bookchin (1983 [1974]), Tim Ingold (2016 [1986]) and Thomas Piketty (2020).

1.1.1 The Commodification of Social Relations: State as an Arena of Conflict

In *The Great Transformation* (hereafter *TGT*), Karl Polanyi provides an insightful account of the relationship between economy and society. He documents how until the nineteenth century the economy was embedded in society, but that in the eighteenth century liberal thought had begun to emerge and the autonomization of economic science stimulated the belief that, for the economy to function economically, it was best for its regulation to be left to the free market mechanisms of supply and demand. Polanyi shows how this was a great liberal illusion, especially with respect to the hoped-for equilibrium between society and economy. The disembedding of the market economy gradually led to the creation of fictitious commodities, three of which Polanyi identifies as labour, land and money. Liberals argued that '[t]he elements of industry had to be on sale' (Polanyi 2001 [1944], p. 78). *TGT* shows the interactions between the enclosure movements, which made land available for upscaled agriculture and industry and the creation of a reserve army of labourers to work in the (new) industries. Polanyi also explains how money, originally meant as a means of exchange and store of value, gradually became detached from its social origins and began to function as unregulated capital.

TGT's really original contribution centres on the documentation of the intimate political and social character of the struggle to promote and resist the commodification of land, labour and money. Polanyi demonstrates the prominent role of the State in the rise of mercantilism in regulating embedded land and labour. He also shows the complexity of the struggles as the State becomes an arena of conflict between the movement for commodification (of social relations) and the counter movement by diverse societal actors reacting against this trend. He further understands the potentially contradictory character of counter movements that, because of their interference with the market, disorganize industrial life and endanger society in other ways—as illustrated by the rise of protectionism, Fascism, or the New Deal; (see Section 1.1.4).

1.1.2   The History of Mutual Aid: from Tribal Solidarity via Village Communities to Medieval Cities

Polanyi's analysis logically leads us to two prominent anarchist authors, namely Peter Kropotkin and Murray Bookchin, who adopt a *longue durée* perspective[2] from early humanity onwards on sociality and different forms of social relations. Their analysis of the development of society, communities and ethics is a key element in our ambition to establish a more politically relevant connection between social innovation and socio-political transformation. Indeed, social innovators often appeal to communities as cornerstones of social innovation and contemporary democratic governance. Communities are often protagonists of solidarity ethics and act as a lever to re-balance individualism and collectivism.

Peter Kropotkin's analysis of the history of sociality begins with the animal world, of which the 'first humans' were part. Kropotkin, as a zoologist and a pioneering evolutionist with profound knowledge of Darwin's work, explains how many of Darwin's contemporary and later interpreters misread Darwin as explaining evolution purely in terms of survival of the fittest, thereby not registering the key role of 'mutual aid' as an engine for building society.

Kropotkin explains how the study of the life of animals up to the end of the nineteenth century shows that '[s]ociability is as much a law of nature as mutual struggle' (Kropotkin 1914 [1902], p. 5). He elucidates how early humans were part of the natural world and had to find, like animals, a balance between mutual struggle and mutual aid (Kropotkin 1914

[1902], p. 77). Since the very beginning of their prehistoric life, humans used to agglomerate into gentes, clans or tribes, maintained by an idea of common descent and by worship of common ancestors (Kropotkin 1914 [1902]):

> As we go back in the palaeo-ethnology of mankind, we find men living in societies – in tribes similar to those of the highest mammals; and an extremely slow and long evolution was required to bring these societies to the gentile, or clan organization, which, in its turn, had to undergo another, also very long evolution, before the first germs of family, polygamous or monogamous, could appear. Societies, bands or tribes – not families – were thus the primitive form of organization of mankind and its earliest ancestors. (Kropotkin 1914 [1902], pp. 79–80)

Yet, Kropotkin also sees the dark sides of tribal solidarity when its survival is threatened. He cites anthropological research that mentions infanticide, abandoning old people, blood-revenge, etc., but also shows how these are limited in extent and regulated by customary practices. Indeed, they can be related to the need of the tribe to survive as a whole (it has mouths to feed) and to protect itself against other tribes or against its own members who do not respect the tribal rules. An important factor of evolving solidarity bonds is the tension introduced by the appearance of the separate family amidst the clan relations. 'A separate family means separate property and accumulation of wealth' (Kropotkin 1914 [1902], p. 113).

The transition from tribal 'savagery' to the 'barbarism' of village community life in the Western world (some 2000–3000 years ago) emerged from a combination of population growth, changing ecological conditions, intertribal wars and (resulting) mass migration. This did not destroy mutual aid but transformed it (Kropotkin 1914 [1902], p. 119). It led to the emergence of the village community. In Europe, this would remain the main form of collective togetherness for centuries, until the rise of the medieval city. The village community came with new or strengthened forms of organization: it recognized and emphasized the independence of the family and gave more freedom to personal initiative and to the union of people of different ancestry, which created community bonds strong enough to oppose 'dominative tendencies'. The private property of families only concerned movable property. Land was common property (of the tribe, village community, or divided among the families). Private property was introduced much later and very gradually, mainly under the influence of Roman principles (occupation by or contact with Rome).

Village communities developed local forms of political organization. Of course, all of this was predicated upon a strict gender division, compounded by forms of 'naturalized' social hierarchy.[3]

It is important to specify that village communities arose before serfdom was imposed and that they kept their judicial powers for centuries—even when they became submitted to a feudal lord.[4] Indeed, the village community became a union for common culture, guaranteeing fair shares in common land, organizing mutual support in diverse forms. It was a 'new' pre-political institution (after the clans or gentes) that had emerged from the turmoil of climatological changes, intertribal wars and massive migrations. Individual families, driven away from their clans and threatened by these turmoils, had found new forms of unity in the village community, which took the role of confronting natural catastrophes, possible oppression by hostile tribes, emergent feudal rulers, etc.; procedures were established to settle quarrels, feuds, offence of community rules, rebellion and murder or theft. Chapter 4 of *Mutual Aid* concludes with an appealing evocation of how village communities recovered social life through collective agriculture, domestic industries, roads linking communities and so on. It also shows how political roles such as the regulation of land use rights and judicial mediation were developed and how customary law was elaborated and dominated legal systems through modern times.

In many ways the success of the village communities also enabled the growth of villages into cities and the transformation of local power into the feudal system and, later, the making of the State. Why, then, did the (Western) world in its next stage of development not evolve into a large brotherhood or collectivity of village communities? Why did it instead become transformed into a landscape of social and spatial relations in which warrior bands became politically dominant, only countered by growing cities? Is it naive to confirm Kropotkin's hypothesis that the very peacefulness of the barbarians, certainly not their supposed warlike instincts, enabled their subsequent subjection to military chieftains (Kropotkin 1914 [1902], p. 155)? Coalitions between entrepreneurial villages, families and 'hirdmen of the armed brotherhoods' often became the basis of wealth creation and accumulation that would soon promote the formation of more cities. But wealth creation and power building were only two sides of the legacy of the village community socius. The third side was the establishment of justice, grown from the desire and struggle of the masses to maintain peace and find justice—first established in customary laws and later in juridical and ruling institutions—which also became the basis for the authority of kings and feudal lords.

Kropotkin argues that 'the deeper we penetrate into the history of early institutions, the less we find grounds for the military theory of the origin of authority' (Kropotkin 1914 [1902], p. 159). The rise of the medieval cities that remained independent for decades (or sometimes even centuries) occurs as an articulation between on the one hand the search for power of the emergent feudal lords who sought to subordinate land labourers and craftsman, and on the other hand the drive of village communities to protect and consolidate their autonomy. Villages fortified, grew, agglomerated, stood up against the lords.[5]

City organization took on a concrete form: it came with the creation of fraternities, the establishment of a city jurisdiction firmly rooted in customary law, as well as the setting up of an autonomous defence system against invaders and ambitious feudal lords. 'Defensors' (Lords, Bishops, …) tried to impose themselves on the cities, also claiming financial tributes, but the cities frequently rejected and replaced them with elected *defensors* with only limited rights but great duties (to protect the 'immunities' of the towns, defend their liberties and so forth). Village communities became integral constituents of the towns or continued their life on their own, yet often as part of the economic hinterland of the city. The creativity of the medieval city was not based on

> the genius of individual heroes, not in the mighty organization of huge States or the political capacities of their rulers, but in the very same current of mutual aid and support which we saw at work in the village community, and which was vivified and reinforced in the Middle Ages by a new form of unions, inspired by the very same spirit but shaped on a new model—the guilds. (Kropotkin 1914 [1902], p. 113)

The medieval city was a double federation composed of all householders united into small territorial unions (the street, the parish, the section) and individuals united by oath into guilds according to their professions; the former being a product of the village community origin of the city, and the second a subsequent formation called to life by new conditions. These conditions, conducive to creativity and social innovation, were destroyed by the rise of mighty States that centralized political power and mobilized armies of serfs (Kropotkin 1914 [1902]).

Guilds were organized according to a craft or a profession, but also often for the pursuit of a project (such as a sea voyage or building and maintaining a cathedral). Guild statutes stipulate that guilds are brotherhoods based on solidarity, brethren are bound by duties of solidarity and mutual aid, especially in case of disease or death; they also detail self-jurisdiction rules to deal with quarrels or conflicts. Guilds reflect an emergent class structure in the cities: guilds of serfs, guilds of freemen, or of both serfs and freemen. Craft and trade guilds survived for centuries, even when cities lost their status as the main socio-political entity in Western society.

1.1.3   The Rise of the Centralist State: the End of Mutual Aid?

The rise and consolidation of village communities resulting in the creation and proliferation of medieval cities show the repeated (at first dispersed and then more institutionalized) attempts of people to reconstruct society on 'the old basis of mutual aid and support' (Kropotkin 1914 [1902], p. 224). Why, then, did the medieval city model not successfully resist the growing power of feudal lords and growing State power? Why did it succumb to these powers instead of further developing networks of autonomous cities such as the Hanseatic League? Kropotkin identifies three factors explaining this lack of resilience.

First, he mentions the privileges of the 'burghers' that excluded other inhabitants from 'the commonality' and contributed to the emergence of oppressive trusts (Kropotkin 1914 [1902], p. 218). This exclusion extended to the peasants living in the villages surrounding the cities. In many cases, this led to noble lords mobilizing the peasants and the second-rank citizens to revolt against the cities and enabled the lords to take power. Several cities made agreements with noble lords to leave them the control of peasants outside the city walls in exchange for recognizing the city charter and becoming co-burghers. This often spurred revolt among peasants against the privileged cities.

A second factor, Kropotkin argues, is that the economic base of cities consisted of commerce and industry and neglected agriculture. The resulting incapacity to feed the population led to urban poverty and social conflicts in the city (Geremek 1997), with inherent tensions between the Church and city authorities regarding poverty relief (Dewitte 2002). This factor reinforced tensions and prepared fertile ground for revolts both inside and outside the cities.

The third factor was the rise of statist ideology and centralist political organization as dominant socio-political discourses. This heralded a return to Roman law and modes of governing. More or less starting in the twelfth century (for example, at the University of Bologna) and for two or three centuries,

> [it was] taught from the pulpit, the University chair, and the judges bench, that salvation must be sought for in a strongly-centralized State, placed under a semi-divine authority; and that one man can and must be the saviour of society, and that in the name of public salvation he can commit any violence. (Kropotkin 1914 [1902], pp. 220–221)

Consequently, '… the old federalist principle faded away, and the very creative genius of the masses died out' (Kropotkin 1914 [1902], p. 221).

Resistance to the rising power of omnipotent monarchs in the fifteenth and sixteenth centuries largely coincided with the rise of the Reform movement and Protestantism. The Protestant movement was a revolt against the coalition between the Church and the lords, but also against the exploitation of the village communities by the feudal lords. During the German Peasants' War of 1525, for example, the Swabian League demanded the return of communal lands to the village communities and the abolition of feudal servitudes (Kropotkin 1914 [1902], p. 225). Massive revolts by peasants were often cruelly oppressed. Central States 'systematically weeded out all institutions in which the mutual-aid tendency had formerly found its expression' (Kropotkin 1914 [1902], p. 226). The State sought control of all relations between citizens and no unions or associations beyond the State would be accepted. This principle was reinforced by the French Revolution. The State's absorption of all social functions 'necessarily favoured the development of an unbridled, narrow-minded individualism. In proportion as the obligations toward the State grew in numbers the citizens were evidently relieved from their obligations towards each other' (Kropotkin 1914 [1902], p. 227). The State, bit by bit, came to substitute mutual aid.

This does not mean that mutual-aid institutions and practices have disappeared in modern society. First of all, the resistance of communal institutions to the rising centralism was real. In many countries and regions, the enclosure movement was delayed or even reversed. Peasants kept their communal institutions, albeit with diminished power, until deep into the eighteenth century. Communal resources, shared labour and solidarity with impoverished households also persisted in community life. The centuries long, cyclically returning struggle of peasants gradually led to the abolition of serfdom and feudalism. But, recognizing the Polanyian ambiguity of counter movements, this transformed the dependency relations between lord and serf into, on the one hand, domination of the proletarian worker by the capitalist entrepreneur and, on the other hand, the citizen by the autocratic State. Regal State and capitalist interests increasingly converged under mercantilism; the tumultuous transition from autocratic to parliamentary kingdoms in many ways reinforced the alliance between State and Capital.

Second, with the rise of the centralist State, guilds were gradually destroyed or became a field of symbolic memberships. But this destruction fed the movements for new solidarities, especially among the industrial proletariat. In late eighteenth-century England, going against the law forbidding any unionization beyond the State, workers created friendly societies, burial clubs, secret brotherhoods, etc., which later developed into the creation of unions in all trades. After a period of relative liberty (as of approximately 1825), union members were prosecuted under the Master and Servant Act, strikes were repressed, and the legal system acted as class justice in a crude way (Kropotkin 1914 [1902], pp. 266–277). But this repression could not stop the rise of the unions, which would become (a little more than a century later) one of the most powerful social forces in what had become a market society.

Third, along with unionization and the continuous struggle with State and capitalist powers, came the rise of political associations 'whose activity many workers consider as more conducive to general welfare than the trade unions, limited as they are now in their purposes' (Kropotkin 1914 [1902], p. 270). Kropotkin explains that 'all great political movements were fought upon large and often distant issues, and those of them were the strongest which provoked most disinterested enthusiasm' (Kropotkin 1914 [1902], p. 270). The rise and impact of socialism should be interpreted from this perspective. But this institutionalization and centralization of mutual-aid agency, fighting for decent pay, housing, health care and education, should not close our eyes to 'the countless societies, clubs, and alliances, for the enjoyment of life, for study and research, for education, and so on, ... are another manifestation of the same ever working tendency for association and mutual support' (Kropotkin 1914 [1902], p. 279). It is important to note that the rise of unions and socialism went along with the emergence of the 'Economie Sociale'. Unions were built from the bottom up and federated; this also held for the cooperatives, bakeries, food and supply shops, health insurance, saving banks, etc.— established as particular agencies within socialist and other solidarity movements (Swedberg 1994).

1.1.4 Persistent Commodification and a Strangling Monetary Policy Diluting Solidarity Mechanisms

Let us at this point return to Polanyi's analysis of *TGT*. It is during the last quarter of the nineteenth century and early twentieth century that the big conflicts between the movement towards commodification and market regulation of the economy (and therefore of the attempts by increasing parts of society, and counter movements, to restore the societal character of labour, land and money) culminated. Liberalism involved maintaining the four pillars of the national and international order: the international gold standard, a balance of powers in international relations, subsistence wages for workers (creating poverty among the proletariat and feeding deflation), and a private market in land.

The liberal system showed increasing signs of crisis in the twentieth century. The counter movement grew with trade unionism. The crisis in the international gold standard was precipitated by the costs of the First World War, which was nonetheless handled with attempts to maintain it by deflationary policy measures that cut wages and public spending that triggered the Great Depression. The 1920s and 1930s saw three reactions to the crisis of liberalism: fascism, socialism and the New Deal. Fascist regimes came to power by using the rules of young democracies or just overthrowing them through physical and military might (such as the Weimar Republic in Germany, and the Popular Government in Republican Spain) or exploiting the poor outcomes of the First World War (the case of Italy, creating a ground for renewed expansionism under Mussolini). These regimes usually provided decent social protection for the 'faithful own folks' but were merciless in eradicating their opponents.

Polanyi shows that these fascist regimes can be considered as (outcomes of) counter movements against market-driven regulation of society. What then should have gone differently to ensure that a new countervailing movement would indeed reverse the commodification movement and (partly) restore the embedment of the economy in a society based on solidarity mechanisms?

For Polanyi, the rise of Keynesianism (though he did not use the term) was quite promising. Adepts of the French regulation school explained the main features of Fordism and Keynesianism as one of the most stable periods in the history of contemporary capitalism (the 30 glorious years of post-war growth until the mid-1970s). The regulation school examined this in terms of a temporary equilibrium between regulation and accumulation dynamics that was secured through an institutionalized compromise between capital and labour (Table 1.1). This reflected the inherently hierarchical character of the Fordist production system that granted significant financial benefits to core workers in core sectors accompanied by weak forms of economic participation in, for example, the Administrative Council, in exchange for a hierarchical, top-down production system with a far stricter division of labour than under Taylorism (Gambino 2007 [1996]). In addition, as an organizer of the mixed economy, the State became a conglomerate of powerful agencies, a bureaucracy capable of redistributing income and welfare services through the welfare State.

The stability of Fordism depended significantly on a stable international monetary order. The Bretton Woods agreement, replacing the Gold Standard, provided a relatively manageable monetary system based on a gold–dollar standard. However, this system was flawed by the growing contradiction between the need to export dollars to other economic powers to create global demand, and the need to maintain surpluses in the US balance of payments to fund the export of dollars. This contradiction led Nixon to abandon the gold–dollar exchange rate in 1971, helping to precipitate stagflation in Western Europe and leading to severe pressure on the wage–labour relationship, social security and welfare (Vandenbroucke and Moulaert 1983).

The instability of the international monetary and trade system, spurred by the so-called oil crisis, combined with a slowing down of productivity increases and a consolidating spatial division of labour, put the production system under high pressure. The Fordist accumulation regime gradually transformed into a post-Fordist accumulation regime, based on just-in-time manufacturing, flexible employment regimes, and weakened labour rights. The dissolution of labour rights was partly compensated for by the recognition of so-called 'human well-being' rights (access and

Table 1.1   Fordist regime of accumulation and mode of regulation: a characterization

Regime of accumulation	Mode of regulation
(a) Mass production: - Large-scale production units - Technology: mechanization and automation, production lines, non-flexible fabrication tools	(a) Wage–labour relation: wage compensation for productivity gains, collective bargaining, social protection, role of the State
(b) Leading sectors: automotive, electrical appliances, petro chemistry Typical market form: monopolistic competition	(b) Competition: monopolistic competition regulated by the state and international agreements
(c) Distribution of produced value: - Class: wages linked to productivity; finance capital's income - Social groups: importance of professional organizations and public agents - Public functions: focus on physical and social infrastructure, social protection	(c) Forms of State regulation: - Public spending for economic stability and anti-cyclical policy - Redistribution of income and wealth (within the middle and working class) - Regulation of market mechanisms - Participation in international negotiation and regulation
(d) Structure of social demand: health, education, social protection	(d) Integration into the international regime of free trade and the monetary system of Bretton Woods (fixed exchange rates, IMF, World Bank, etc.)
(e) Social and spatial division of labour: - Hierarchy of regions and cities	

Source: Moulaert 2000.

protection rights for alter-abled people, gender equality, …). With the advent of neoliberalism in the 1980s, the role of the State was gradually reduced from the Keynesian-welfare national State to an entrepreneurial post-national workfare regime. This promoted supply-side innovation, subordinated welfare measures to labour market flexibility, hollowed out the national State and relied on partnerships to deliver economic and social policy. The neoliberal subordination of social policy to the increasingly pervasive norms of competitiveness and active labour market policies meant that only the 'really excluded' should benefit from public resources (Piketty 2020).

1.1.5   The (Post-)Industrial Urban Society: Is It Still Possible to Restore the Bonds of Solidarity?

In *The Limits of the City*, Murray Bookchin (1983 [1974]) explains the transformation of the medieval commune first into the bourgeois city and then into the metropolis and megapolis. In the latest edition of this book, Bookchin seeks to understand the role of State sociality in urban life today. The lead mechanism in his analysis is best summarized by the following:

> If the mere extension of commodity relations can be said to have transformed the medieval commune into the bourgeois city, the factory may be singled out as the agent which gives the city its structural form and its social purpose. By the word 'factory' I mean more than an industrial enterprise: the factory is the locus of mobilized abstract labour, of labour power as a commodity, placed in the service of commerce as well as production. Accordingly, the term applies as much to an office building and a supermarket as to a mill and a plant (Bookchin 1983 [1974], p. 75).

Several forces that led to centralized States overruling the power of the medieval cities also explain their decline and transformation into industrial and post-industrial cities. These forces include: the proletarianization of the masters and apprentices at work in the less capitalized workshops; the growing exploitation of rural labour by urban *entrepôts* [warehouses]; the stepwise integration into the international economy; the building of city networks with an inter-urban division of labour as well as severe inter-urban competition and so on.

A key factor in the capitalist urbanization of society was the enclosure movement, which peaked in the early nineteenth century, not coincidentally one of the fiercest periods in the rise of capitalism. Its social and ethical devastation is still grossly underestimated even today. Disinvested people fled from the rural lands, villages and small cities to big cities, soon transforming into big agglomerations whose fringes housed the slums of the heyday of Western industrialization.

A second principal factor of the capitalist urbanization of society, partly due to the first, is that traditional communal solidarity bonds were broken; life circumstances degraded to hunger and homelessness, urban migrants were robbed of their land, condemned to selling their labour power at a less than subsistence level, initially deprived of any ethics of communal solidarity. In their later stages of development, the restored social relations of (post-)industrial cities became ruled by a mix of bureaucratic and market practice. This is reflected in the bureaucratic organization of the trade union; the rise of the impersonal supermarket and mass merchandizing; and the replacement of popular forms of community decision-making (such as the assembly and town hall meeting) by a mechanical electoral process that transfers policy formulation to preselected representatives whose roots in the community are tenuous or non-existent. According to Bookchin, in the early revolutionary phase, bourgeois society could claim with some justification that it sought to liberate individuals from the shackles of caste, religious superstition and authoritarian corporatism. Today, in its late, distinctly corporate phase, the same society retains the individualism of its early period to create isolated egos without personality (Bookchin 1983 [1974], p. 87). Individuals lose individuality and conform to market logic by seeking to excel in achieving labour market feasible skills and acting as 'conscious' consumers of heavily marketed goods. Already in the 1980s, this was a passé image. Metropolises were structured by peri-urban housing patterns, car-driven transportation networks, overconsumption of natural resources (land, water, air, 'raw' materials, ...) and lack of respect for other natural inhabitants of the (peri-)urban lands.

Bookchin's chapter 'The Limits of the Bourgeois City' summarizes the impoverishment of the social, political and cultural 'capital' of the metropolis and the megacity:

> If history tells us that the divine city once competed with the earthly city for ascendency over the human spirit, today it can be reasonably said that both have been pre-empted by the institutionalized and depersonalized city; for the Metropolis is no work of man or god, but rather of the faceless bureaucracies that had acquired control over society and denature the human spirit. ... The bodies that touch each other in the subways, in the elevators of the great buildings, and in the streets are surrounded by a psychic field of indifference. (Bookchin 1983 [1974], pp. 105–106)

And:

> Any desire to communicate is muted by the unspoken understanding—a psychic equivalent of the 'social contract'—that the urbanite's personality can only retain its integrity in a mass society by a sullen inwardness pop, a dumb impregnability to contact with the mass. The segmented roles that bureaucratization imposes on the ego are resisted by the myth that the blasé indifference to the world at large is a mode of withdrawal from a homogenized society; the anomie that pervades the crowd can only be exorcised by clinging to one's

sense of privacy and by tending to one's own affairs. (Bookchin 1983 [1974], p. 106)

This characterization of human interaction in the large city illuminates the collective discouragement to participate in political life that has been dominated (since Fordism) by top-down, science-driven and public management-style administrated factories and bureaucracies. Decentralization and neighbourhood or community involvement in public politics and governance have become very hard to achieve in this context. The deep desire among many urbanites and social groups to restore bonds of solidarity, ethical principles reflected in customary law, participation and co-production that are innate to human nature is very hard to achieve in conditions of bureaucratized anonymity, socio-ecological alienation and de-politicization.

1.1.6   Historical and Contemporary Examples of Socially Innovative Political Movements

From Polanyi we learned that movements that rose in reaction to the growing marketization of society can take different forms over time and that their intentions are often not fully materialized. To understand the interaction between Social Innovation (SI) and social political transformation, it is important to observe the moments in history at which socially innovative and political movements arose, what triggered them, and what the connections between the two were. Let us refer to some emblematic historical and contemporary examples of such counter movements and how their life cycle developed.

Frequently cited and quite relevant are the guilds and fraternities in Western medieval cities. Their impact on the medieval urban polity and governance was very significant. To a certain extent, they introduced customary law, mutual-aid principles and cooperative economy into municipal charters and regulations. These facilitated what we would call organic burgher democracy, including a high level of solidarity among masters and merchants and their families, but a rather philanthropic attitude towards apprentices, rural-to-urban migrants and so forth. This movement countered the attempts of emerging feudal lords taking control of the lands, but in so doing watered down into an urban economic hierarchy of cities, with masters and merchants accumulating capital, exploiting rural workers in the urban hinterlands and apprentices and rural migrants within the cities. Notwithstanding, the organic burgher democracy (and the interrelations between sociality and polity therein) provides a source of inspiration for exploring affinities between social and political movements today.

The rise and institutionalization of the 'Economie Sociale' was probably the most remarkable trajectory of socially innovative practice supported by scientifically based thought in the nineteenth and early twentieth centuries. A social political movement that involved many social fields, it laid the basis for the nineteenth-century cooperative economy that influenced polity and politics, thereby seeking to counter the exploitative factory system and the liberal politics of the time (i.e. the era that Polanyi pinpointed as the emblematic moment at which the economy sought to disembed itself from society and give free range to commodification). Workers' movement leaders, unionists, cooperatives, enlightened entrepreneurs, social economists, sociologists, political activists, leaders, all found each other in the construction of a long-lasting trajectory combining new cooperative enterprise models, new legislation, institutional structures, education and research. This facilitated the gradual build-up of a social economy as an alternative for the wildcat capitalism of industrialization at the time (Moulaert and Ailenei 2005; Defourny and Nyssens 2013; Moulaert and MacCallum 2019).

The social and emancipation movements of the post-Fordist era also provide emblematic experiences of socially innovative political counter movements. These involve at least three subsequent waves of social mobilization: (1) the 'radical emancipation wave' of the 1960s–70s, (2) the neighbourhood and community (re-)development period (1980s–2000s) and (3) the ongoing 'social and solidarity economy', which received a new impetus with the financial crisis of 2008. Their periodizations overlap and their agendas are complementary. The radical emancipation movements focused on fighting the hierarchy of corporate capital, dismantling the authoritarian State and challenging patriarchy in most top-down institutions in the social welfare, education, health and penitentiary system. The neighbourhood and community (re-)development movement targeted urban neighbourhoods in decline due to industrial restructuring, threats by large development projects, and worsening ecological conditions. This movement quite soon also adopted sustainability and food security strategies, thereby providing the basis for current social and ecological movements. The new social and solidarity economy movement targeted relief for the economic victims of the post-Fordist restructuring and the

2008 financial crisis. This last period saw part of the social economy instrumentalized in the process of rationalizing the welfare State, including privatizing parts of welfare State services. At the same time, the transition movement and diverse types of grassroots movements (dealing with housing, food security, gender and ethnic equality) began to take root across continents and communities. Furthermore, technological and economic innovation systems literature opened up to SI as a complementary dimension of innovation and stressed the importance of synergies between technological, social and organizational innovation and analysed the social impact of innovation strategies and policies (Fagerberg 2006).

The dependency of many of these movements on the State and public money is striking and exacts a high price in terms of managerial codes to follow. Emancipation and collective education initiatives became institutionalized and in many countries were turned into subsidized training organizations that have to live up to the norms of public management and adaptive governance.

1.2   Contemporary debates on social innovation and socio-political transformation

This section considers the contemporary debates on the relationships SI, social change, political life and socio-political transformation today. First, we consider the dualities in SI thought and practice in the neoliberal era. Next, we examine to what extent the political remains embedded in the economic, how this has led to contradictory interpretations of the political, and tempered opportunities to make the political re-emerge from its 'public management' crisis.

1.2.1   Breaking through the Duality in Social Innovation and Political Thought and Practice

The significance that various mainstream strategy and policy documents accord to SI varies greatly. Nonetheless, they tend to interpret it in economic, indeed often in narrowly market-economic, terms. This commonality is strongly influenced by management science, innovation economics and a micro-economic interpretation of SI strategies. While SI certainly has economic aspects, stressing them too strongly can easily lead to a reductionist interpretation of SI and its potential. This focus becomes clear in the way mainstream strategy and policy documents explain how SI initiatives should address social problems, the overly organizational view of innovation in social relations, and the privileging of firms as the (potential) carriers of social innovation. The last feature prioritizes social businesses over social movements as vehicles for social innovation and thereby not only misrepresents the functioning of the social economy but also reduces the field of SI practice.

This biased approach to the relationship between economy and society is characterized by the recurrent tendency in much of the cited literature to consider the social economy as an aggregation of individual social enterprises. Such a conception of the social economy—and therefore also the socially embedded economy as a whole—does not adequately reflect its advanced degree of institutionalization, its market dynamics, its typical relations of production and cooperation, or its articulation with the wider social world. This economistic and reductionist account of the social economy has three mutually reinforcing weaknesses. First, it ignores the distinctive macro-economic aspects of SI as an interactive ensemble of practices. Second, it neglects the economic aspects of social innovations that are not immediately economic in their objectives, such as the democratization of the educational system, the pursuit of gender equality, or the psychiatric liberation movement (Chambon et al. 1982). And, third, its emphasis on economic agency pushes other types of socially innovative agency, including those in the social economy, into the background. These weaknesses are reflected in a superficial understanding of the relations between social change, social transformation and social innovation. Overall, this narrow view of SI promotes a 'caring liberalism' that privileges social enterprises as the key agent for social change and regards the economy as the primary sphere of social life.

Our approaches to SI break through this dual relationship between social enterprise and social innovation as supported by the mainstream literature. We counter its general neglect of the macro-social dimensions of social innovation (albeit acknowledging that it at times addresses SI agency and processes at different spatial scales and with regard to different levels of collective action). We remedy this neglect by indicating how different analytical entry points can be combined to facilitate a better understanding of the potential complementarity between SI as a series of bottom-up strategic initiatives with local roots; as a coherent set of top-down but 'enlightened' institutional reorganizations that could enable and promote bottom-up initiatives at different spatial levels; and in so doing, demonstrate how these form natural ingredients for improved political democracy. We particularly explore two tracks of SI following the Fordist period in the advanced capitalist economies: (1) SI based on a rediscovery of the social economy; and (2) SI as a multifaceted movement for social emancipation and human development. Both tracks have developed in the context of new socio-political dynamics that call for more proactive institutional arrangements. They converge in the rise of community-based and grassroots-initiated initiatives oriented to a much wider spectrum of human needs essential to human development than those considered by earlier generations of social enterprise, State-led social protection agencies, social movements and organizations. This is shown in our concern for social and political transformation as opposed to technological innovation (Moulaert and Nussbaumer 2007; Godin 2012; Van den Broeck et al. 2019).

SI oriented to human development is not concerned primarily with business innovation but with the diversity of human needs that must be met for human development to materialize. Accordingly, SI research aims to promote innovation in social relations and socially innovative strategies in various spheres of society. Thus, its ontological perspective affirms the social, spatio-temporal and substantive contingency of social relations and the correlative human capacities for social transformation. Its epistemology is likewise sensitive to the inevitable dialectics of struggle between forces pursuing radical SI oriented to social emancipation and those seeking to maintain an asymmetrically organized social order biased towards profit-making, efficient markets, and business-friendly social relations. In this lies also its (contested?) potential for (socio-) political renewal.

1.2.2   Social Innovation: Historical (Dis-)Continuity between Practice and Holism

Social Innovation analysis is characterized by a discontinuity between the 'old' theorists of social change (from the end of the nineteenth century or even earlier centuries up to the 1960s or 1970s), who did their research in a much more pre- or proto-disciplinary period or style, and the 'new lighters' in SI analysis (from the 1970s onwards) (as explained by Moulaert and MacCallum 2019; Moulaert et al. 2013). These 'new lighters' do not form a cohesive group of scholars defending the same SI ontology—the ontology of SI that can solve societal problems at different spatial scales. Although several contemporary analysts continue to work in the 'old' tradition, most of them are now more inclined to use a more micro-logical, partial, or practice-oriented approach. This re-orientation is linked to a view of SI as a key vehicle in 'caring liberalism' that favours social enterprise as the agent for social change within the boundaries of the market society and treats the economy as the primary sphere of social life. Our principal argument is that to give SI analysis a coherent onto-logical and epistemological status, as well as its necessary methodological tools, the 'old' social change analysis needs to be reunited with the more practice-oriented analyses of the last three decades. Most of our own work should be situated in this 'return' movement.

The French intellectuals of the 'Temps des Cérises' can be considered the main actors of a turning point that allowed the 'old' theories of social change to shed their light on the new 'social innovation' approaches. These intellectuals participated in a debate of wide social and political significance on the transformation of society and, in particular, on the role of the revolts by students, intellectuals and workers. They were also interested in the socio-political meaning of particular social innovations. Subsequently, Chambon, David and Devevey (1982) explained how SI satisfies specific needs thanks to collective initiative, which is not synon-ymous with State intervention. In effect, they argue that the State can act, at one and the same time, as a barrier to SI and as an arena of social inter-action that can stimulate SI originating in the spheres of State or market. They stress that SI can occur in different types of communities and at various spatial scales, but is conditional on processes of consciousness raising, mobilization and learning.

Contemporary debates in SI analysis should focus on a number of unre-solved issues and key challenges (Moulaert and MacCallum 2019). First of all, SI analysis should put more energy into reconstructing the different trajectories in SI research by better connecting the influence—or lack thereof—of the old schools on the new schools. This will also require an examination of the relationships between the history of thought and prac-tice in institutionalism and that of collective action and social movements. Indeed, as we have seen in Section 1.1, the role of institutions in society has changed significantly; institutions have become mainly free market protectors, rather than custodians of equity and general well-being.

Therefore, SI research should focus first of all on *changing social relations* through creating new forms of collaboration and reconfiguring the institutional forms that have (at best) neglected and (at worst) directly created or exacerbated the needs and problems caused by the externalities of technological and economic innovations (such as social exclusion or environmental degradation) (Moulaert and MacCallum 2019, p. 31).

Second, SI innovation research faces one of the persistent challenges in social and political science research: the so-called micro–macro tension. 'Macro' or 'social' or 'collective' is more than the sum of micro or individual behaviour. In between these stand issues like (and the terminology varies according to the schools of thought) externalities, public choice, collective action, institutionalization, societal and community evolution or revolution, culture and cultural change, local-global, scalar dynamics, ... Though most new SI initiatives and research are situated at the micro-level, they cannot be addressed accurately without taking the 'macro' dynamics into account. This is why our analysis of SI initiatives at the local or the individual organization level examines the scalar dynamics, the (de)institutionalization processes, the networking processes involving diverse agents and institutions, the cultural life, etc. These are essential in evaluating the relationships between SI and social political transformation.

Third, and this is not contradictory to a more holistic approach to SI (Moulaert and Mehmood 2020), specific distinctions need to be made between approaches that take into account disciplines, epistemological and methodological perspectives, and fields of application. In fact, confronting diverse approaches with each other will contribute to distinguishing the various dimensions of the holistic picture of a SI process. For example, in the tradition of the Social Innovation Action Research Network, Moulaert and MacCallum distinguish two subcategories (as differentiated by Parés et al. 2017): the 'geographical' perspective focuses on territorial, human and community development, emphasizing the spatiality of social relations (e.g. Moulaert and Nussbaumer 2007; MacCallum et al. 2009; Moulaert et al. 2005; Moulaert et al. 2013; Trudelle et al. 2015; Van Dyck and Van den Broeck 2013); and a 'political science' perspective primarily focuses on how SI reconfigures democratic governance, particularly in terms of political discourse (Eizaguirre et al. 2012; Leubolt and Weinzierl, 2017; Novy and Leubolt, 2005) and vis-à-vis the State (e.g. García 2006; Pradel Miquel et al. 2013; Martinelli 2013; García and

Vicari Haddock 2016; Lévesque 2013; Gonzalez and Healey 2005). These approaches have considerable connections and overlaps. For example, in both the geographical and political science perspectives, governance is inextricably linked to territoriality, and institutional dynamics are central in leading to transformational change. Taking this into account, differences between approaches are due to disciplinary focus expressed in specific themes and socio-spatial relations rather than any particular ideological or methodological basis (which also explains the common cross-citation between literatures; van der Have and Rubalcaba 2016; Galego et al. 2021).

Despite their often very practice-oriented approach, many contributions to the SI literature of the last few decades advocate or show the need for a more societal approach to SI agency, its institutions and cultural expressions. This concerns especially the literatures addressing relationships between governance and socio-political systems. In these contributions, experiences materializing the ethics of mutual aid and community building occupy a significant role. But are these ethics of thought and practice strong enough to also inspire solidarity-based socio-political transformation? Can SI initiatives, networks and movements be factors of macro-transformations?

1.2.3   The Macro-Socio-Political Meaning of Social Innovation

Since hominids developed language and invented tools, social progress has been premised on social creativity, discoveries and inventions, and their translation into successful innovation. What seems *new* in the contemporary world is the self-reflexive emphasis on, and high regard for, innovation and its role in economic development and competition, political reform and revolution and social progress more generally; and, relatedly, the self-description (justified or not) of individuals, groups, organizations, institutional orders, and even whole societies as innovative rather than traditional or conformist (cf. Nowotny 2008). This is said to create the conditions for a de-centred politics, no longer strongly State-centric and no longer coupled to a mixed economy in which the State is the principal means to compensate for market failure. This allegedly creates the conditions for more individualistic or networked forms of social mobilization, innovation and entrepreneurship, and for pursuing non-commodifiable use-values and models of human organization beyond the division of labour.

This provides an initial entry point into the relationship between *macro-social* developments and an increasing self-reflexive interest in SI and its implications for human emancipation and economic and political organization, going well beyond the sphere of 'civil society' or the life-world. This can be taken further if we consider how social movements react to changes in functional systems that fetishize reified social logics such as competitive market exchange at the expense of human interaction and sociability. A modern classic in this regard is, of course, Karl Polanyi's thick historical description of how 'society fought back' against the commodification of land, labour and money in the nineteenth century (2001 [1944]), which we examined in Section 1.1. This involved a lot of SI— cooperatives, trade unions, friendly societies, workers' reading circles, working-class 'building societies' and so on. It produced a whole proletarian social movement and public sphere that could be seen as socially innovative organizationally and as oriented to human emancipation (Negt and Kluge 1993). Polanyi also discussed how fascism, communism and social democracy represented different ways of embedding Fordism into new economic, political and social orders (Polanyi 2001 [1944]).

Under Atlantic Fordism, as Carpi (1997) notes, there was little room for the social economy to socially innovate because there was no pressure to do so; alienation of social groups and individuals under Fordism were often of a different kind and connected to other types of social belonging than those defined by production relations and division of labour (Massey 1995 [1984]). While emancipation movements addressing different issues were mushrooming, the existent social economy institutions (Cooperatives, Mutualities, …) were mainstreamed within the Fordist system. The new movements followed a diversity of institutional trajectories ranging from becoming annexes of political parties, NGOs, loosely funded associations, etc. to anarchist action groups refusing any institutional form or funding.

The crises in the Fordist and neo-mercantilist economic development models in the 1970s and 1980s led in some cases to a neoliberal turn based on the principle of 'more market, less State' as if the mixed economy had failed and, in others, to interest in economic, political and social arrangements that depended neither on the anarchy of the market nor the hierarchical control of the sovereign State but extended public–private partnerships, expanding networks and reliance on the solidarities of civil society. It is in this context that the social economy has been (re-)

discovered from a wider multi-dimensional SI perspective, addressing community building and mutual-aid relationships, interpersonal respect and cooperation, bottom-up and bottom-linked democracy, ... But 'resetting' the social economy was only one aspect of the socially innovative initiatives and processes that pervaded Fordist society in the late 1960s and early 1970s. Fordism also enabled path-breaking struggles around non-class antagonisms: greater gender equality, women's liberation, the rise of anti-pedagogy, breaking down of the walls of psychiatric clinics, the criticism of clientelism in the Fordist political regimes, and the call for more direct democracy and citizen participation (see Offe 1985; Buechler 1999). This was also the period when the excess burden of capitalism on the ecological system and socio-cultural relations in communities were revealed and criticized. In later years, this led to a revival of the literature on utopia and how they could play a role in social emancipation, community building and social transformation (Achterhuis 1998).

In line with the evolution of Fordist society, the *social economy* was transformed in a way that shows certain elective affinities with the transition towards post-Fordism. Carpi has observed a broad congruence between the dynamic of post-Fordism and the dynamic of a social economy in terms of three trends. The first was the emergence of an alternative movement seeking both new forms of economic organization (democratic) and new market niches (natural and ecological goods, ideologically committed bookshops, etc.). The second was the growing weight of the service sector (*tertiarization* of the economy), the development of flexible production systems and the externalization of functions on the part of firms, which have propelled the growth of small businesses and the feasibility of productive organizations in expanding activities without any great investment. Third, a restructuring of State activity and the externalization of public service management, stimulated by the fiscal crisis and conservative ideological-political assaults, with the aim of 'rationalizing' the welfare State, has created new opportunities for the social economy to expand but unfortunately quite often within a regulatory regime based on new public management (NPM) modes of governance submitting social innovation to micro-economic criteria (Jessop et al. 2013). At the same time, the recomposition of State action in social and economic affairs and the technological and economic transformation under way have created a growing number of problems and unsatisfied needs (unemployment, social exclusion, territorial decline) that have affected civil society and local authorities. Consequently, alternatives are sought outside the capitalist sector and the State (Carpi 1997, p. 256).

The search for alternatives considers problems faced by peripheral or semi-peripheral economic, political and social spaces that cannot engage in 'strong competition' and therefore run the greatest risk of losing out in the zero-sum 'game' (struggle would be a more appropriate term for such encounters) for external resources (cf. Jessop 2000). In such cases resorting to a social economy grounded in local social movements and concerned with empowering the poor, deprived and underprivileged, seems to provide a more effective solution. It does so by developing a more self-sufficient economy that might be able to re-insert itself into the wider economy or secure the conditions for a viable, local, solidary economy within a local community, rebuilding solidarity relations across all its existential fields (Cassinari and Moulaert 2014). Thus an expanded, recalibrated and socially embedded social economy could help to redress the imbalance between private affluence and both public and private poverty, to create local demand, to re-skill the long-term unemployed and re-integrate them into an expanded labour market, to address some of the problems of urban regeneration (e.g. in social housing, insulation and energy-saving), to provide a different kind of spatio-temporal fix for small and medium-enterprises, to regenerate trust within the community and to promote empowerment.

In this sense, and against the logic of capital, the social economy prioritizes social use-value that in a competitive market may (but usually does not) have a high valorization potential. It seeks to re-embed the organization of the economy in specific spatio-temporal contexts oriented to the rhythms of social reproduction rather than the frenzied circulation of digitalized finance capital. It also challenges the extension of the capitalist logic to other spheres of life such that education, health services, housing, politics, culture, sport and so on are directly commodified or, at least, subject to quasi-market forces. Indeed, extending the social economy provides a basis for resisting capital's increasing hegemony over society as a whole. For it demonstrates the possibility of organizing economic and social life in terms that challenge capitalist 'common-sense'.

Such innovation is clearly social in form and content and represents a serious challenge, at least ideationally and normatively, to the complementary logics of market and State. It revalorizes, in particular, the idea of social networks and moral communities, of reciprocity and solidarity, of negotiated consent and unconditional commitment. Therefore, we could say that the recent developments in the social economy have integrated several of the 'other' dimensions of SI such as the innovation in social relations in societal and community spheres, human development targets, interpersonal and social ethics, socio-political empowerment and so on. These developments have shown that, to organize communities and develop strategies to satisfy socio-cultural needs, economic modes of coordination do not have to correspond either to the criteria of NPM, or the micro-efficiency of the private firm. In addition to understanding this, it is paramount to underline that the social enterprise modes of 'doing economics' most of the time do not conform to those dictated by the logic of global competition. Equally important is highlighting, again, that the social enterprise is only *one* type of SI actor among many others, including cultural organizations, popular education organizations, neighbourhood associations and social services, autonomous living communities and so on. Although always having to work with economic resources of various natures, these actors have their own objectives, social ambit, modes of cooperation and co-production and are innovative partners in rebuilding sociality within this market society.

For all types of SI actors and institutions, key to the success of SI are new forms of social learning oriented to the production of knowledge as an intellectual commons organized around collective, problem-oriented learning. Such forms of social learning require a shift from today's dominant ethics framed by hegemonic imaginaries of finance-dominated capitalism (however 'financially innovative' and 'expertise-based' they might be) and of the 'knowledge-based economy' (with its privileging of intellectual property rights) towards an emphasis on solidarity-based learning through sharing and cooperation. While in general this reorientation of innovation away from the prioritization of profit-oriented, market-mediated economic expansion depends on a wide range of bottom-up initiatives meant to revalorize a diversity of social use-values, it also requires a wide range of institutional supports that can connect these initiatives, share good practice and provide broader orientations. Such institutional supports should not be imported by, for example, an enlightened State, but should grow from experiences of bottom-up and bottom-linked governance driven by ethics of mutual aid, interpersonal respect (active listening, empathizing …) and co-production (see Chapter 2). Too many innovative institutionalization processes fail because of a lack of trust between partners, the pursuit of personal benefits without considering the common good, or control and retaliation by private capital interests.

The most appropriate framework for this form of politico-institutional (re)organization is a multi-spatial (not merely multi-level or multi-scalar) pattern of subsidiarity. In such a framework there should be as much local initiative and autonomy as possible and as much trans- or supra-local support as necessary to enable an equitable, ecologically sustainable social order. A compelling argument for this approach (apart from the moral virtues of SI and the solidary economy, and the social benefits resulting from their practices) is the urgent, imminent threat of hyper-individualism to energy, food, water and environmental security but also to human dignity and reciprocal respect between human beings. This is both the biggest challenge and the greatest chance for a reorientation of our economic, political and societal arrangements (see Jackson 2009; Victor 2008). Collective (re)learning of solidarity ethics in family, school and peer group learning is essential to meet this challenge.

1.2.4 Core Concepts: Governance; Polity/Politics/Policy/the Political; SI and Social Spheres

This section introduces some core concepts that inform the analyses in the reflection and the debate chapters of this book. First, the meaning of governance and its modalities is discussed. Governance is a broad concept that refers to different ways of coordinating social action in complex situations. There are four ideal-typical modes of governance: exchange (exemplified by the market), command (exemplified by organizational hierarchies and the State), networks (illustrated by public–private partnerships) and solidarity (unconditional commitments based on membership of a real or imagined community). Each has a different logic. Markets involve self-interested pursuit of individual goals in an anarchic process that has no agreed aggregate goal (it operates post hoc as an invisible hand). Command operates through a hierarchical authority that sets a substantive collective goal to be attained through bureaucratic procedures. Networks operate through horizontal communication to agree on a common objective among stakeholders through continuous negotiation that changes the objective as circumstances change. Solidarity involves unconditional commitments to help members of the community through mutual aid (cf. Kropotkin 1914 [1902]). Each mode has its own mode of failure: market failure involves the inefficient allocation of scarce resources to competing goals; State failure involves the failure to achieve collective goals; network failure often leads to social and economic inefficiency; and solidarity failure amounts to unrequited love or betrayal. The existence of governance failure leads to hybrid governance in which the weaknesses of each are compensated by other modes of governance, e.g. the State governs the market; public–private networks overcome the separation of market economies, civil society and State organizations; and solidarity is invoked when all else fails. Metagovernance of this kind also fails, of course, because there is no master metagovernor in the sky with a clear perspective on complex and/or wicked problems and how they can be solved. In addition, metagovernance is multi-spatial. It needs to operate across different territories, places, scales and networks, and secure spatio-temporal fixes that displace and defer contradictions, dilemmas and paradoxes. All contributors to this Dialogue share this approach to governance, its hybridity, the importance of governance and metagovernance failure and the need to develop democratic forms of governance in the interests of bottom-led multi-spatial metagovernance.

The second set of core concepts is the quadruplet of the polity, politics, policy, the political and their relation to civil society. The polity describes the ensemble of institutions that characterize the official political regime and its supportive institutions. Politics is the set of social practices that attempt to shape the exercise of power in a political regime. The polity and politics can be democratic or authoritarian and there can be different forms of each. Policy comprises the set of specific policies and their overall articulation that political actors apply in a political regime. The political regime, in following Gramsci, comprises political society + civil society, i.e. hegemony protected by the armour of coercion (Gramsci 1971, p. 263). For example, both are regarded as sets of social relations rather than merely a set of institutions without agency; in this view, the boundary between political society and civil society is analytical rather than real. In terms of modes of governance, civil society can be seen as an ensemble of partnerships and solidarity, political society as dominated by the hierarchy of command, and the modern economy as dominated by a set of profit-oriented, market-mediated exchange relations. The struggle over SI concerns the attempt to hegemonize the political regime to be responsive to bottom-led governance mobilization and to pursue policies that support innovative practices in different territories and places across different scales. This requires the reworking of political society–civil society relations to make bottom-led social movements and bottom-linked democracy experiences by such movements become legitimate partners in political mobilization for social and political transformation. This can be contrasted with current trends towards authoritarian Statism, in which top-down State power is the dominant mode of politics and policymaking, and power is exercised in the interests of political elites and their allies.

The concept of 'the political' contrasts to the triplet polity/politics/policy. The latter refers to the empirically verifiable architecture of organizing the public sphere—that is, the rules, principles, practices and institutions of governance. In contrast, the notion of 'the political' refers to the radical heterogeneity and conflicts that cut through any social order and the constitutive role of political action to suture the public sphere. In this sense, the political is constitutive. It is also prone to fail to fully make the public sphere coherent. While it cannot be directly observed, it can be discerned in moments of rupture or interruption, when 'those who do not count' interrupt the given order and stage/demand egalitarian inclusion. Such 'political' events emerge 'at a distance' from the State and aim at transgressing/transforming the existing instituted order.

A third set of core concepts concerns the organization of social formations into distinct social spheres. These reflect the division of social labour in terms of different functional systems and their interdependence. Examples would be the environment, technology, market economy, the socio-cultural world, the social economy, politics, law, education, religion, welfare, housing and mass media. Social agents can be identified in terms of their role within a given system and/or in terms of identities that cross-cut their belonging within one or another system. The latter include gender, generation, ethnicity, sexual orientation, spatial belonging, migration status and so on. Class can be defined in terms of place in the division of labour and power within the economy or extended to include its correlative position in civil society and political society.

Social innovation is defined here as a combination of the satisfaction of human needs, the building of solidarity-based social relations and empowerment towards socio-political transformation. It concerns the ability of social agents to pursue creative and innovative strategies and build organizations in any given field and to connect different fields in pursuit of these strategies. In contemporary societies, the dominant articulation of fields is set by the political economy of capitalist accumulation; in contrast, this book is concerned with promoting the critique of political ecology, which includes taking account of the environmental impact and countering the individualist ethics of capital accumulation when pursuing social innovation. This can be considered a utopian perspective that aims to replace the ideological defence of the status quo and depends on the mobilization of counter- and sub-hegemonic resistance to the hegemonic or dominant order. But equally so it can be considered as the ultimate change to go against the strategic trends of planetary destruction, including the absolute dissolution of solidarity bonds across social groups, families and individuals.

This review of concepts indicates the terrain on which the dialogues of the three interlocutors are located. As readers will discover, they have different yet complementary perspectives on the relevance of these concepts. Frank Moulaert prioritizes bottom-led governance and Social Innovation. Erik Swyngedouw places more emphasis on broadening the political sphere to accept radical social agents as legitimate partners in the political system and to limit the political power of dominant economic and political agents. And Bob Jessop is more inspired by Gramsci's concern with the historically contingent articulation of political society and civil society and with the modalities of metagovernance. All three main contributors are concerned with the possibilities and limits of Social Innovation in building movements of socio-political transformation.

1.3   Reflection and debate: three viewpoints on social innovation and its socio-political change potential

The reflection chapters of this book expose the viewpoints of the three authors with respect to the politically transformative capacities and potential of Socially Innovative practices and movements, with each author using a particular theoretical and conceptual lens yet with ontologically common ground. The objective is to compare and confront, both through separate reflection pieces and a dialogical encounter, different approaches with respect to a shared objective, i.e. contributing to our understanding of and articulating with galvanizing politically performative possibilities that may trigger socio-political transformation on the basis of experiences, practices and possibilities garnered by socially innovative practices.

1.3.1   A Common Diagnosis of the Present Situation

The three reflection pieces share a diagnosis of the present situation. First, there is a growing disdain for democratic and inclusive political arrangements symptomatically present in the lure of autocratic and xeno-nationalist populist movements and a general retreat from participation in political life. Second, there is an increasing transformation of the State to a system of expert-management of a broadly neoliberal order for which there is ostensibly no alternative. Put differently, the State has turned into a bureaucratic-expert dispositive that manages the existing socio-economic order. Third, the authors point to the intensifying forms of multiple deprivations and exclusions (partly galvanized by the decline of a universal welfare State) and weakening of social equity, which have contributed to a growing unequal triaging of life with widely different opportunities and conditions for different people. Fourth, the sedimentation of an overall macro-economic market logic that sutures public and private life, combined with a growing individualism, segmentation and fragmentation at the level of the subject, has led to a deeply penetrating commodification of everything and contributed to the further disintegration of a common social bond. Fifth, the proliferation of a wide range of unfulfilled human desires and needs (ranging from access to adequate housing, stable employment, secure health services, accessible education, a nurturing ecological milieu, etc.) and the retreat of the State in securing these services for all has intensified precarity, social exclusion and socio-ecological inequality.

These symptoms of the present condition have spurred a series of responses and experimental modes of organizing socio-ecological life in ways that either remedy, intersect with or seek to transform the socio-ecologically disintegrating forces at work. There is indeed no shortage—across the globe—of emblematic, innovative and inspiring new forms of social organization that seek, in a variety of ways, to enact new forms of solidarity and community, to empower citizens politically, to build new modalities to produce and deliver common goods and experiment with more inclusive forms of deciding, governing and implementing policies or other actions. The question that is at the forefront of our dialogue is the extent to which the proliferation of prefiguring new forms of social engagement may open avenues, strategies and possibilities for nudging socio-political transformation in an emancipatory, egalitarian and socio-ecologically inclusive manner.

1.3.2   Three Reflections and their Affinities

Frank Moulaert develops his reflection on the basis of actually existing bottom-linked governance examples that bring together SI initiatives and local government actors and agencies. Mobilizing the wide-ranging academic literature on SI and territorial development and reconstructing the research genealogy that moved from SI to bottom-linked governance, his reflection insists on the political potential that resides in social practices and their capacity to transform the instituted order. While recognizing the uneven impact and success of such initiatives, he clearly discerns in some of these bottom-linked initiatives a performative effect in terms of nudging or transforming local government in the direction of governance arrangements that are conducive to solidifying and supporting innovative social practices.

The key insight here is indeed that changing social relations and socio-ecological configurations through experimental and innovative practices *do* have a political significance and may lead to enabling governance transformation that becomes structurally embedded in the governmental apparatus, thereby co-constituting new socio-political regimes. The example of the recent governance shift in Barcelona is of course foregrounded as an emblematic example of the socio-political regime shift that was set off by the anti-austerity (Indignados) movement, but on the basis of a wide and heterogeneous panoply of socially innovative movements and practices that dotted the Barcelona social landscape for many years. The latter formed a fertile ground for translating local practices not only into political demands, but also in changing the institutional landscape itself.

Successful examples of bottom-linked governance nonetheless remain fragile. This is particularly noticeable at the local level, at the scale of the local authority. The case study of Buurtontwikkelingsmaatschappij Antwerpen (BOM)—Neighbourhood Development Association (Antwerp)—testifies to both the possibilities of bottom-linked initiatives to fertilize socio-political change, but remain nonetheless vulnerable to changes in the political regime, something that local initiatives do not have a great sway over. In addition, to the extent that they are successful at somewhat transforming local socio-political arrangements (as the case of Barcelona demonstrates), their capacity to upscale and universalize such socio-political transformation remains difficult if not impossible.

The key perspective that Frank Moulaert puts forward insists on the political importance of prefigurative social practices and how indeed changing social practices may, in the right circumstances, transform the institutional choreography of (local) governance arrangements. The emphasis here is clearly on the centrality of socially innovative practices.

Erik Swyngedouw, for his part, shifts the focus of attention from fore-grounding social practices to considering the question of the political. The latter, so the argument goes, is the terrain on which the struggle for political-institutional change is fought. In other words, the political unfolds in articulation with prefigurative social practices, but cannot be reduced to the latter. The 'political' stands for the heterogeneities and antagonisms that cut through any social order and seek to transform the existing community. The political is, therefore, symptomatically discernible in forms of acting that disrupt or interrupt any given order. In doing so, 'the political' demonstrates the empty ground upon which any society is instituted. Moreover, 'the political' affirms the inegalitarian inscriptions that mark any given instituted order, and seeks to transform that order in more egalitarian and inclusive manners. The political is marked by forms of acting in public that demonstrate the wrongs inscribed in the social order, and through interruptive acting, seeks an ega-libertarian transformation of the existing order.

This perspective affirms the importance of prefigurative socially innovative practices, but argues that the terrain for socio-political transformation requires considering the political as a semi-autonomous domain through which the struggle for change unfolds. To take the case of Barcelona, the existence of bottom-linked socially innovative practices was indeed vital, but institutional-political change accelerated through forms of political acting performed by the 'Indignado' movement. Moreover, these forms of political acting might transcend the local scale and have, under certain conditions, the possibility of scaling up to nudge socio-political change at regional, national or supra-natural scales.

Bob Jessop, taking a broadly Gramscian perspective, seeks another path to consider the articulations between social and political practices, and how they form particular configurations of governance. He emphasizes that the mobilization of socially innovative practices to nurture socio-political transformation has to rely primarily on networked relations and practices of solidarity rather than on markets or hierarchy and command-based governance configurations. The former, then, can form the basis of a counter-hegemonic struggle. This involves a struggle on a variety of fronts to create a different, working-people-based, vision of a solidarity-based society and the creation of counter-hegemonic movement capable of transforming the status quo.

This analysis permits considering the governance arrangements and varieties of organization that might nudge bottom-linked socially innovative practices on a path that fosters socio-political organization. Following Samuel Becket's dictum from *Worstward Ho!*, 'Ever tried. Ever failed. No matter. Try again. Fail again. Fail better', Bob Jessop considers the importance of recognizing failure, and learning how to fail wisely. His contribution seeks to bridge the duality between 'the social' and 'the political' that the other two contributions highlight.

Taken together, these three reflections provide a wide-ranging and multi-perspectivist vision of the political possibilities promised by bottom-linked socially innovative practices, and set the scene for a dialogical encounter between these three distinct, but interrelated, views.

1.4 The way forward: a dialogical encounter

The dialogical encounter between the three authors, which took the shape of a public debate in 2019, brings to the fore the multifaceted nature and variegated potential detected in new forms of social engagement's ability to propel, stimulate (or, depending on their perspective, demand, and ultimately provoke) socio-political transformation in a socio-ecologically inclusive and emancipatory way. The point of tension between the three viewpoints (which as aforementioned share a similar diagnosis and common objective but differ in mechanisms and analyses) has to do with pinpointing exactly *how* democratizing political change occurs (under what circumstances, through which means and to what final end?). The three interlocutors have different ways of approaching the underlying questions that drive this point of tension: in spite of the plethora of socially innovative initiatives why do many people and social groups no longer believe in politics or see their agency in reinventing the 'political'? And why do social political experiments not culminate in powerful political change movements? Bottom-linked governance is an attempt to make this symbiosis happen, but is it really working? Another question underlying the main point of tension, and arising in the conversational debate, is: why do social movements not prioritize in their agendas the political/social nexus (making the political more social and vice versa) and truly counter the individualist ethics of capital accumulation? Bringing these questions closer to home, and touching the very *raison d'être* of many academics, activists and policymakers present during this dialogical encounter, is the question of why liberal northern Europeans engaging in social movements do not engage in politically subversive initiatives (or vice versa?).

In answering these questions in the debate, the interlocutors analyse the space/time dynamics determining the real transformative potential of bottom-linked governance practices. Do these practices risk diluting down into technocratic de-politicized answers? Do they reproduce or strengthen the logic of capital? Frank Moulaert asserts that it is only through social dynamics at interactive spatial scales that social political transformation will be triggered; the dynamics seeding into bottom-linked governance practices (experimentation based on mutual-aid ethics, democratic learning, networking, etc.) hold the potential of *transforming* the working of local governance (recognizing of course that State dynamics do not stop at the level of local government). Erik Swyngedouw argues that political events rarely translate into a politicizing procedure that ends in an institutional change and transformation. The key ingredients for social political transformation are no longer clear: we no longer live in the nineteenth and twentieth centuries where a political event turned into an emancipated sequence of social and political actions leading to, for example, the welfare State. Sustaining the politicizing sequence (shifting from a localized to a universalizing procedure) is problematic because these social mobilizations lack effective political strategies for *lasting* political change. Bob Jessop, often positioning himself in the 'middle', points to the differences in opinion between his colleagues regarding what a politicizing procedure means. The place/space dimension here is again key, as the structures of the State must be taken into account in understanding the potential impact of SI strategies. Drawing on Poulantzas (distinguishing between struggles to design the State/struggles within the State/those at a distance from the State), he points to the importance of redesigning the State by affording opportunities for local authorities to support socially innovative initiatives and of ensuring horizontal linkages to guarantee a transfer of best practice beyond the local.

The interlocutors then turn to discussing the relevant themes of reinventing democracy, the re-politicization of society and self-emancipation. They agree that experimental innovative social practices are essential for political transformation; they approach the specificities and emphasis of what the political therein actually *is* from different angles. Frank Moulaert draws on the history of democracy building and the variety of socially innovative experiences, showing how bottom-linked governance is in a way essential for a new political movement and for re-politicizing society; how experiments in social and political practice are conflictual, often unsuccessful, involve co-learning, but nonetheless are *key* in reinventing democracy. Erik Swyngedouw details the dynamics of the emancipatory process (the notions of equality and freedom being historically continuously re-constituted), entreating that in order to reinvent democracy we can't be afraid of failing (because all emancipatory attempts *will* fail). Bob Jessop highlights the centrality of flexibility within a governance system, creating space for a strong, pluralistic and heterogeneous civil society to debate and be self-reflexive in order to reinvent democracy (a process which will not, in any case, fit everything for all time in a given locality but is in constant flux). This civil society is under threat of increasing Statization or commodification.

Finally, the conversation is propelled by an urgency that bites to the heart of the matter: what are the implications of this diagnosis, not only on an institutional level but also on a personal and interpersonal one? Undergirding the exchange on the elements of economic and political transformation and the examples of the transitions of social movements into political organizations (such as the case of Barcelona) is a search for identifying the main actors involved in mobilization, political action and subversion for political transformation. Frank Moulaert offers no black and white answer, but points to what history has shown us: it is in situations of advanced exploitation or social/political/economic alienation that we find fertile ground for social political movements that transform systems. Bob Jessop argues that a class-based interpretation of the social bases of innovation risks ignoring the centrality of powerful, wider forms of solidarity and networking. Erik Swyngedouw brings it close to home for those in the audience saying 'I am very much on Žižek's side when he says that the key problem today is the fact that we know very well what the situation is (ecologically, socially, in terms of capitalism, exploitation, etc.) (see Swyngedouw, Chapter 5, p. 112) but we act out our everyday lives as if we do not know.' The debate thus turns to addressing the absence of political subjectivation and the deconstruction of the different components of the 'we'; how to avoid the reproduction of de-politicized bottom-linked social movements; the post-democratic political and personal ethics. Solidarity features as a response to the felt impasse (otherwise we would just be living 'off the privileges of being—in our case—well-paid white male intellectuals in relatively neat institutions' (see Jessop, Chapter 5, p. 113)), but must be coupled with a willingness to engage in real-world problems. Recognizing our differing societal roles and specific functions in the social world, the debate concludes with a call on the audience to break the mould of being passive onlookers and to wholeheartedly engage—on all levels—with the challenge of making emancipatory social movements scale-up to ensure a politically trans-formative impact in today's world.

1.5   Overview of the book

Following this introductory presentation, each interlocutor presents a reflection chapter exposing their analysis of the key question addressed in this book. In Chapter 2, 'Bottom-linked governance and socio-political transformation', Frank Moulaert situates bottom-linked governance in territorial social innovation research, presenting and drawing lessons from several bottom-linked governance experiences and emphasizing their potential in bringing about socio-political transformation.

Chapter 3, 'Is political transformation possible in an age of post-politiciza-tion?' by Erik Swyngedouw questions the socio-political potential of SI innovations, arguing that although they may be essential for stimulating emancipatory social change, they are politically non-performative if not articulated with politicizing movements. The chapter calls for a shift in focus away from a sociological lens and towards the theoretical, intellectual and practical elements of political processes and their interaction with new social forms.

Chapter 4, 'Exploring the dilemma between self-emancipation and self-responsibilization' by Bob Jessop analyses modes of governance (forms of failure and attempts at metagovernance) and uses conjunctural analysis to argue that when civil society is mobilized through solidarity and networks, the logic of politics is transformed into 'the art of the possible'—whereby civil society can become a means of self-emancipation in an ecosocialist order.

Chapter 5, 'Debate: a dialogical encounter on the potentialities of social innovation for social political transformation' provides accessibly reformulated minutes of the debate, where the three thinkers interact on issues regarding the politicization of social movements and reinventing the political.

Chapter 6, 'Towards socially innovative political transformation' formulates suggestions for transforming the socio-political system by better reconnecting social and political concerns in society. Can socially innovative practices and institutions (e.g. built according to the insight of bottom-linked governance) be powerful to this purpose?

Notes

1. The debate took place on 4 April 2019 as part of the International Module in Spatial Development Planning (an interactive PhD training programme in which PhD and research Master's students present and discuss their research with leading academics from all over Europe) organized by the Planning & Development (P&D) Research unit at the Department of Architecture, Faculty of Engineering Sciences, KU Leuven.
2. As defined by the *Oxford English Dictionary*, 'A perspective on history that extends deep into the past, focusing on the long-standing and imperceptibly slowly changing relationships between people and the world which constitute the most fundamental (and hence the least questioned or analysed) aspects of social life, and incorporating findings from disciplines such as climatology, demography, and physical geography. Later also more generally: the long term in historical discourse, as opposed to current or recent events.'
3. Only exceptionally gifted or materially well-off women had a significant role in medieval society. Hildegard von Bingen is probably one of the most prominent female personalities of the early and middle Middle Ages. She was

one of the greatest female artists and intellectuals of the Western Mystical Tradition and as an abbess became confidante of popes and kings (Fox 2002).
4. Similar, often earlier, developments of village communities occurred outside of Europe.
5. As Kropotkin wrote: 'The movement spread from spot to spot, involving every town on the surface of Europe, and in less than a hundred years free cities had been called into existence on the coasts of the Mediterranean, the North Sea, the Baltic, the Atlantic Ocean, down to the fjords of Scandinavia; at the feet of the Apennines, the Alps, the Black Forest, the Grampians, and the Carpathians; in the plains of Russia, Hungary, France and Spain' (Kropotkin 1914 [1902], p. 163).

References

Achterhuis, H.J. (1998). *De Erfenis van de Utopie*. Ambo.

Bookchin, M. (1983 [1974]). *The Limits of the City*. Harper Row.

Buechler, S.M. (1999). *Social Movements in Advanced Capitalism*. Oxford University Press.

Carpi, J.a.T. (1997). The prospects for the social economy in a changing world. *Annals of Public and Cooperative Economics*, 68(2), 247–279.

Cassinari, D. & Moulaert, F. (2014). Enabling transdisciplinary research on social cohesion in the city: the social polis experience. In E. Silva, P. Healey, N. Harris & O. Van den Broeck (eds), *The Routledge Handbook of Planning Research Methods*, 414–425. Routledge.

Chambon, J.-L., David, A. & Devevey, J.-M. (1982). *Les innovations sociales*. Presses Universitaires de France.

Defourny, J. & Nyssens, M. (2013). Social innovation, social economy and social enterprise: what can the European debate tell us? In F. Moulaert, D. MacCallum, A. Mehmood & A. Hamdouch (eds), *The International Handbook on Social Innovation: Collective Action, Social Learning and Transdisciplinary Research*, 40–52. Edward Elgar Publishing.

Dewitte, A. (2002). Poverty and poverty control in Bruges between 1250 and 1590. *City*, 8(2), 258–265.

Eizaguirre, S., Pradel-Miquel, M., Terrones, A., Martinez-Celorrio, X. & García, M. (2012). Multilevel governance and social cohesion: bringing back conflict in citizenship practices. *Urban Studies*, 49(9), 1999–2016.

Fagerberg, J. (2006). Innovation: a guide to the literature. In J. Fagerberg, D.C. Mowery & R. Nelson (eds), *The Oxford Handbook of Innovation*, 1–25. Oxford University Press.

Fox, M. (2002). *Illuminations of Hildegard of Bingen*. Simon and Schuster.

Galego, D., Moulaert, F., Brans, M. & Santinha, G. (2021). Social innovation & governance: a scoping review. *Innovation: The European Journal of Social Science Research*, 1–26. https://doi.org/10.1080/13511610.2021.1879630.

Gambino, F. (2007 [1996]). A critique of the Fordism of the Regulation school. *The Commoner*, 12, 39–62.

García, M. (2006). Citizenship practices and urban governance in European cities. *Urban Studies*, 43(4), 745–765.

García, M. & Vicari Haddock, S. (2016). Introduction to special issue: housing and community needs and social innovation responses in times of crisis. *Journal of Housing and the Built Environment*, 31, 393–407.

Geremek, B. (1997). *Poverty: A History*. Blackwell.

Godin, B. (2012). Social innovation: utopias of innovation from c.1830 to the present. *Project on the Intellectual History of Innovation Working Paper*, 11, 1–5.

Gonzalez, S. & Healey, P. (2005). A sociological institutionalist approach to the study of innovation in governance capacity. *Urban Studies*, 42(11), 2055–2069.

Gramsci, A. (1971). *Selections from the Prison Notebooks*. Lawrence & Wishart.

Ingold, T. (2016 [1986]). *Evolution and Social Life*. Routledge.

Jackson, T. (2009). *Prosperity without Growth: Economics for a Finite Planet*. Earthscan.

Jessop, B. (2000). Globalization, entrepreneurial cities, and the social economy. In P. Hamel, M. Lustiger-Thaler & M. Mayer (eds), *Urban Movements in a Global Environment*, 81–100. Routledge.

Jessop, B. (2015). *The State: Past, Present, Future*. Polity.

Jessop, B., Moulaert, F., Hulgård, L. & Hamdouch, A. (2013). Social innovation research: a new stage in innovation analysis. In F. Moulaert, D. MacCallum, A. Mehmood and A. Hamdouch (eds), *The International Handbook on Social Innovation: Collective Action, Social Learning and Transdisciplinary Research*, 110–130. Edward Elgar Publishing.

Kropotkin, P. (1914 [1902]). *Mutual Aid: A Factor of Evolution*. McClure Philips & Co.

Leubolt, B. & Weinzierl, C. (2017). Social innovation to foster social development? *Journal für Entwicklungspolitik*, 33(2), 4–12.

Lévesque, B. (2013). Social innovation in governance and public management systems: toward a new paradigm? In F. Moulaert, D. MacCallum, A. Mehmood & A. Hamdouch (eds), *The International Handbook on Social Innovation: Collective Action, Social Learning and Transdisciplinary Research*, 25–40. Edward Elgar Publishing.

MacCallum, D., Moulaert, F., Hillier, J. & Vicari Haddock, S. (eds) (2009). *Social Innovation and Territorial Development*. Ashgate Publishing.

Martinelli, F. (2013). Learning from case studies of social innovation in the field of social services: creatively balancing top-down universalism with bottom-up democracy. In F. Moulaert, D. MacCallum, A. Mehmood & A. Hamdouch (eds), *The International Handbook on Social Innovation: Collective Action, Social Learning and Transdisciplinary Research*, 346–360. Edward Elgar Publishing.

Martinelli, F., Moulaert, F. & Novy, A. (2013). *Urban and Regional Development Trajectories in Contemporary Capitalism*. Routledge.

Massey, D. (1995 [1984]). *Spatial Divisions of Labour: Social Structures and the Geography of Production*. Macmillan International Higher Education.

Moulaert, F. (2000). *Globalization and Integrated Area Development in European Cities*. Oxford University Press.

Moulaert, F. & Ailenei, O. (2005). Social economy, third sector and solidarity relations: a conceptual synthesis from history to present. *Urban Studies*, 42(11), 2037–2053.

Moulaert, F. & MacCallum, D. (2019). *Advanced Introduction to Social Innovation*. Edward Elgar Publishing.

Moulaert, F., MacCallum, D., Mehmood, A. & Hamdouch, A. (eds) (2013). *The International Handbook on Social Innovation: Collective Action, Social Learning and Transdisciplinary Research*. Edward Elgar Publishing.

Moulaert, F., Martinelli, F., Swyngedouw, E. & Gonzalez, S. (2005). Towards alternative model(s) of local innovation. *Urban Studies*, 42(11), 1969–1990.

Moulaert, F. & Mehmood, A. (2020). Towards a social innovation (SI) based epistemology in local development analysis: lessons from twenty years of EU research. *European Planning Studies*, 28(3), 434–453.

Moulaert, F. & Nussbaumer, J. (2007). L'innovation sociale au coeur des débats publics et scientifiques. Un essai de déprivatisation de la société. In J.L. Klein & D. Harrisson (eds), *L'innovation sociale: émergence et effets sur la transformation des sociétés*. pp. 71–88. Presses de l'Université du Québec.

Negt, O. & Kluge, A. (1993). *Public Sphere and Experience: Toward an Analysis of the Bourgeois and Proletarian Public Sphere*. University of Minnesota Press.

Novy, A. & Leubolt, B. (2005). Participatory budgeting in Porto Alegre: social innovation and the dialectical relationship of state and civil society. *Urban Studies*, 42(11), 2023–2036.

Nowotny, H. (2008). *Insatiable Curiosity: Innovation in a Fragile Future*. MIT Press.

Offe, C. (1985). New social movements: challenging the boundaries of institutional politics. *Social Research*, 52(4), 817–868.

Parés, M., Ospina, S.M. & Subirats, J. (2017). *Social Innovation and Democratic Leadership: Communities and Social Change from Below*. Edward Elgar Publishing.

Piketty, T. (2020). *Capital and Ideology*. Harvard University Press.

Polanyi, K. (2001 [1944]). *The Great Transformation: The Economic and Political Origins of Our Time*. SAGE.

Pradel Miquel, M., Garcia Cabeza, M. & Eizaguirre Anglada, S. (2013). Theorizing multi-level governance in social innovation dynamics. In F. Moulaert, D. MacCallum, A. Mehmood & A. Hamdouch (eds), *The International Handbook on Social Innovation: Collective Action, Social Learning and Transdisciplinary Research*, 155–168. Edward Elgar Publishing.

Swedberg, R. (1994). *Une histoire de la sociologie économique*. Desclée de Brouwer.

Trudelle, C., Klein, J.-L., Fontan, J.-M. & Tremblay, D.-G. (2015). Urban conflicts and socio-territorial cohesion: consensus building and compromise in the Saint-Michel neighbourhood in Montreal. *Canadian Journal of Urban Research*, 24(2), 138–157.

Van den Broeck, P., Mehmood, A., Paidakaki, A. & Parra, C. (eds) (2019). *Social Innovation as Political Transformation: Thoughts for a Better World*. Edward Elgar Publishing.

Vandenbroucke, F. & Moulaert, F. (1983). De bestrijding van de werkloosheid: de bijdrage van Post-Keynesiaanse economen [Dealing with unemployment:

the contributions of post-Keynesian economists]. In W. Van Ryckeghem (ed.), *Macro-economie en Politiek*. Alfen-a/d-Rijn, pp. 167–227, Samson.

van der Have, R.P. & Rubalcaba, L. (2016). Social innovation research: an emerging area of innovation studies? *Research Policy*, 45(9), 1923–1935.

Van Dyck, B. & Van den Broeck, P. (2013). Social innovation: a territorial process. In F. Moulaert, D. MacCallum, A. Mehmood & A. Hamdouch (eds), *The International Handbook on Social Innovation: Collective Action, Social Learning and Transdisciplinary Research*, 131–141. Edward Elgar Publishing.

Victor, P.A. (2008). *Managing without Growth: Slower by Design, not Disaster*. Edward Elgar Publishing.

2 Bottom-linked Governance and Socio-political Transformation

Frank Moulaert

Bottom-linked governance has been recognized as one of the most innovative governance practices stemming from the Social Innovation (SI) 'movement' in urban environments. I argue in this reflection that if we want to work towards a durable transformation of State and civil society relationships, we *need* to take into account local initiatives and how they work with more 'democratic' modes of democracy (i.e. bottom-linked democracy). This is the core statement that I invite my 'sparring partners' in this debate to challenge and/or respond to.

Bottom-linked governance is a concept that grew out of the research on SI, territorial development and socio-political transformation. Meant to transform governance practices of local authorities, to create more socio-politically effective relations between civil society and public authorities at the local level, bottom-linked governance initiatives often had contradictory impacts ranging from radically democratizing (governance) relations between civil society and local governance, to reactions by local authorities neutralizing or mainstreaming SI practices into their 'machinery.'

In this reflection piece, I begin by situating bottom-linked governance in territorial social innovation research, especially the research projects in which I and some of my colleagues here were active. Next, I briefly explain and evaluate some bottom-linked governance experiences and draw some lessons from them, emphasizing their potential in bringing about socio-political transformation.

2.1 Situating bottom-linked governance in territorial social innovation research trajectories

Most of the research on bottom-linked governance was conducted in cooperation between colleagues in the Social Innovation Action Research Network (see Chapter 1, p. 22). In our analysis of socially innovative initiatives within local communities and neighbourhoods, we observed three interconnected main features of SI initiatives and processes.

First of all, the satisfaction of individual basic and collective needs: this includes, for example, housing, decent food, childcare, green healthy spaces and access to social services including health services in one's immediate environment (instead of e.g. having to travel hours to the centre of the city to benefit from such services); it also involves the agency that is essential to satisfy these needs.

The second feature of SI initiatives is the 'improvement' in social relations: I put the word improvement in single quotes because it's a very vague term. When you take into consideration (as Kropotkin has argued at length) the ethics that lie behind building social relationships and bonding, solidarity cooperation and redistribution, mutual aid, then you understand that improving social relationships is about respectful cooperation with collective goals in mind (Kropotkin 1914 [1902]). But of course, you can build solidarity mechanisms for a small community that actually have negative impacts for the social economic position of other communities adjacent or in other areas and so on.

A third feature of SI is empowerment and mobilization towards social and political transformation. We will detail this feature later on, looking at examples of bottom-linked governance from Europe and the USA.

Table 2.1 provides a chronological overview of SI/local development projects funded by the European Commission that serve as a basis for my reflections on this topic (Moulaert and Mehmood 2020). Some say that these espouse a utopian view, being 'idealistic programmes' that we believed could contribute to resurrecting neighbourhoods in cities suffering from manufacturing industry, climate change, restructuring programs, etc. Some of the cases we studied were indeed cases that showed that utopia could be successful, and could have a positive influence on the development of a city (Moulaert 2000). Others showed that yes, we were naive; and since we were naive, we needed a research project that looked at the *real* dynamics of capitalism. That's what we did in 'Urban Restructuring and Social Polarization in the City' (URSPIC; Moulaert et al. 2003): we examined how real estate development and capitalist dynamics of restructuring in a city increasingly reduce the space that is available to urban equity, socially innovative initiatives and the space for the transformation of the social political system. The 'Social Innovation

Table 2.1   Chronological overview of SI/local development projects funded by the EC

Project acronym	Full name/Coordinators	Duration	Context
IAD	Integrated Area Development (Frank Moulaert)	1991–1994	Poverty 3
URSPIC	Urban Restructuring and Social Polarization in the City (Frank Moulaert, Erik Swyngedouw)	1997–1999	FP4
VALICORES	Valorizing Linkages between Private Consultancy and Public Research (Frank Moulaert, Abdellah Hamdouch)	2000–2004	FP5 ACM
SINGOCOM	Social Innovation and Governance in Local Communities (Frank Moulaert)	2001–2005	FP5
DEMOLOGOS	Development Models and Logic of Social Organization in Space (Frank Moulaert, Abid Mehmood)	2004–2007	FP6
KATARSIS	Socially Innovative Strategies against Social Exclusion (Frank Moulaert, Jean Hillier, Diana MacCallum, Abid Mehmood)	2006–2009	FP6 CA
SOCIAL POLIS	Cities and Social Cohesion (Frank Moulaert, Jean Hillier, Diana MacCallum)	2007–2010	FP7 Social Platform

Source: Moulaert and Mehmood 2020.

and Governance in Local Communities' (SINGOCOM; Moulaert et al. 2010) project pushed the pendulum back to the utopian views, to the dreams of changing what was going on in neighbourhoods, putting forward the role of social initiatives, social movements and so on. But it contained a much more *embedded* utopian view of what was possible for the future and took into account what we learned from URSPIC— that there is a real estate market which may leave some cracks for the Commons, for public space, for social economy and as such for social innovative initiatives (Moulaert et al. 2003). The last three projects in the chronology—Development Models and Logic of Social Organization in Space (DEMOLOGOS project 2004–2007; Martinelli et al. 2013; Moulaert et al. 2016), Socially Innovative Strategies Against Social Exclusion (KATARSIS) and Cities and Social Cohesion (SOCIAL POLIS; Moulaert et al. 2013) are more methodological and espouse three different points of view. DEMOLOGOS, in a way, helped us to reflect on the methodology, to analyse urban and regional development trajectories from an interdisciplinary point of view. Here we brought in the role of culture, discourse and institutions much more explicitly in the analysis of spatial development. Whereas in KATARSIS and SOCIAL POLIS we really focused on building models of cooperation between different disciplines, and especially between different practitioners in different social and practice fields (i.e. focusing on transdisciplinarity as forms of cooperation between scientific research and collective action practice). We addressed questions such as: 'How do you work in a joint problematization approach (with actors coming from very different backgrounds) to address problems which everybody recognizes, but for which everybody has a different language, or for which everybody has different ideas for development?'[1]

2.2   Bottom-linked governance

We started using the term bottom-linked governance during the course of the EC Framework 5 Project SINGOCOM (see Table 2.1) to describe governance practices that we observed or took part in within SI initiatives, organizations and networks (see in particular Swyngedouw 2005; García 2006; García et al. 2015; Moulaert et al. 2019). It explained the political dynamics in a number of European cities that could not be understood as 'bottom-*up*' governance. What we were observing was a phenomenon whereby you as civil society organizations have such an influence on the way the local authorities work that they change their style of interacting with you: they change their modes of communicating, they become more open to sharing decision-making and so on. Is that the ultimate transformation of the State we had hoped for? No, it isn't (I will delve into this later) but in any case, it justifies why we shifted from using the term bottom-*up* governance to bottom-*linked* governance. This is not to say that bottom-up governance no longer exists; it can be found—especially in isolated projects, or in projects that follow more autonomous dynamics, less dependent on cooperation with the public sector and that have no further political ambition (but that's another issue).

In our research, we observed several bottom-up governance initiatives with a number of politically ineffective features. We observed a guileless faith that self-governance by itself would have a significant democratization impact on the relationships with the State (or a stronger belief that there is no need for a State); and a somewhat blasé and unreflective conviction that the political system and State apparatus should uncritically adopt or integrate bottom-up decision-making mechanisms of the people (which is another way of defining bottom-up populism).

The analysis of multi-level governance dynamics shows that successful development can rarely be classified as either bottom-up or top-down, but rather as both shaping and shaped by new dynamic forms of conflict and cooperation between civil society and the State, and across scales. What this looks like, in the real world, is things that we see in Toronto, Canada (Manganelli 2020)[2] or in Belo Horizonte in Brazil (until the new president came to power and raised the food programme at a federal level, Rocha 2016).[3] Here we see that new forms of cooperation between bottom-up organizations working for food security have had a significant influence on the way the State is dealing with their quests. Together, they have created new institutions, forms of cooperation, meeting places and agencies for taking measures towards more food security (such as supporting short chain supply, new public procurement procedures for buying local and healthy).

These new forms of democratic governance are interactively built between socially innovative initiatives, activists and organizations. Many of these organizations have actively networked across scales from their very beginning. The 15-M movement in Spain, particularly in Barcelona, is a good example of this: the involved organizations are interacting, they are in conflict with each other, they are negotiating with each other, they are working together. It's from *such a socio-political reality* that we see new forms of what we call bottom-linked governance emerging.

Thus bottom-linked innovation and bottom-linked governance refer to new forms of cooperation across territorial scales in which policies (broadly defined and practised) are not dictated from a particular level of governance, but designed and institutionalized by, and in terms of, the cooperation itself. It is through the cooperation itself that new modes of governance are discovered, defined and institutionalized. A significant part of this institutional innovation is experience-based: it is based on the experience of local initiatives, organizations and local state agencies. An inspiring example is the Groupes d'Achat Solidaires de l'Agriculture Paysanne (GASAP) established in 2006 in Brussels: it negotiated with other partners (local authorities, regional authorities of the Brussels capital region, etc.; Manganelli and Moulaert 2018). It also continued its activities with the change in government in the Brussels region (and this is quite interesting for our research) from a more green ecological-oriented government to a more neoliberal-oriented government, which changed the modes of cooperation between the organizations and the State.

Bottom-linked governance initiatives we studied refer to those initiatives that transform governance practices of local authorities to creative and more socio-politically effective relations between civil society and local authorities at the local level. These initiatives often have contradictory impacts, ranging from radically democratizing (governance) relations between civil society and local governments (as we have witnessed in Antwerp for about 10 years, or as we are seeing in Barcelona over the last decade) to reactions by local authorities neutralizing or mainstreaming SI practices into their 'machinery' (Christiaens et al. 2007; Eizaguirre et al. 2017).

Bottom-linked governance starts from the concern that many new socially innovative initiatives are highly necessary, but that their governance and that of the relevant supportive and re-democratizing State institutions should be developed interactively with their activities and organization. Many bottom-up initiatives *pur sang* that try to link to the local authorities and other organizations have vanished as a consequence of counteractions by the State (for example, the absolute rigidity of the regime, or simply the absolute belief of the State in the neoliberal policy programme—leading them to reject any other initiative that does not fit the neoliberal credo). This means, in fact, that the only type of SI initiatives that are supported in a neoliberal context would be those that contribute to rationalize the welfare State and privatize social welfare services (Oosterlynck et al. 2019).

We should keep in mind that the image of this interaction between socially innovative initiatives and local State agencies is not that of an easy going sweet romance, but a trajectory of co-construction and confrontational moments in which protest and conflict, as well as analysis, co-learning and negotiation, all have a role to play.

2.3 Bottom-linked governance: cases and experiences

A few of the most successful innovations that we have observed are bottom-linked governance practices that were going on in several of the neighbourhood- and community-level development projects (Moulaert et al. 2010; Laino 2012). These include the re-politicization of civic life in Spanish cities (see the case study in Barcelona covered in Chapter 4; Eizaguirre et al. 2017), the construction of 'social regions' (Klein et al. 2017), the development of community-supported agriculture systems (Manganelli 2020) and the politicization of transition towns (Scott-Cato and Hillier 2010). The Spanish quarter in Naples is also a very interesting case to look at—showing a convinced leadership and very dynamic associations often facing political instability, but always in search of interesting connections between the neighbourhood, on the one hand, and the local government, on the other.

From this perspective, the recognition of civil society in multi-scalar governance is important, yet should be considered with care so as to prevent civil society's organizations becoming co-opted or forcing them to 'reduce their imaginative potential, to bridle their creativity or their subversive capacity' (De Schutter 2002, p. 216). It's not just about the connections between these new initiatives and the local State—the higher State levels also play very important roles. We discovered this in the Antwerp case for example: despite the new orientation of European and national authorities to urban development and policies following a neoliberal agenda, the social democrat mayor in Antwerp could have made use of many more cracks and liberties in the system to promote urban equity (Christiaens et al. 2007).

Successful bottom-linked governance comes with the warning 'Handle with care!' In other words: don't become euphoric about its general potential. It's not because an experience works well here and now that it will be the model that will save us elsewhere or in the future.

2.3.1   Buurtontwikkelingsmaatschappij Antwerpen (BOM)

The case I have followed very closely over 20 years is that of a Neighbourhood Development Association based in Antwerp (in Dutch: Buurtontwikkelingsmaatschappij Antwerpen, BOM). Through the 1990s, BOM took on the main agency role in building a neighbourhood development strategy, mainly in north-east Antwerp: it took the city by the hand and led it to form a bottom-led governance approach to neighbourhood development (for example, in cooperation with other organizations, BOM's proposals for Neighbourhood Development Plans for three different neighbourhoods in Antwerp; Moulaert 2000).

Though I will not go into detail of the case here, what I want to emphasize is that the initiative fostered a multi-scalar network or consortium including a mixture of activists, community leaders, scientists, social workers, political figures and so on. The most active community leaders came from the Rijksinstituut voor Samenlevingsopbouw or State Institute for Community Building (RISO); they had a long tradition of criticizing traditional urban policy and gentrification policy and in stressing the role of the social, of culture and the importance of social workers in urban community and city building. There were scientists and activists belonging to the emergent green movement. And there were enlightened politicians: the mayor tolerated what was going on; the Alderman for Social Affairs and Housing at the time (Marc Wellens) was very instrumental in and supportive of the BOM initiative; there was a key network figure working in the Cabinet of the Minister of Science, Schiltz. Later on, the consortium was extended to the business world.

The shift towards a much more neoliberal vision of urban development changed the focus of the European, national and regional city funds. This shift marked a move away from a more integrated view on developing neighbourhoods to a view of development that should be more economic and real estate-driven, and applied citywide instead of at the neighbourhood level only. This view became predominant in the Antwerp city government as of the early 2000s. It was expressed in plain terms by the Alderman of Spatial Planning and Public Works: 'The social workers have had their time to show that they could change the city; now it is time for the economists and the architects to take over, because we [the City government] believe much more strongly in what they will do.' As a result, the bottom-linked governance was given up. We saw how a lot of the creative initiatives of BOM developed in collaboration with city services were mainstreamed, split up and brought up to a higher level in the State system (regional government level and so on).

I also believe that the socio-political and psychological dynamics behind these reactions play an important role. I think some of the city leaders were really frustrated, thinking/saying (but now I am putting words in their mouth): 'The arrogance of this bottom-up organization, taking responsibilities and almost telling the City what has to be done in different neighbourhoods!' I think that unconsciously, or consciously, some of the political figures in the city apparatus wanted to take revenge. One of the leaders of BOM (with whom I co-wrote an article; Christiaens et al. 2007) was persecuted for financial mismanagement, leading her to have to step down. After four or five years, the court decided that she was completely innocent, and had not even made any managerial mistakes. By this point, however, she was gone, and with her—a few years later—BOM had gone as well. So, we can see how a change in the socio-political regime, which is multi-scalar, plays an important role in the opportunities afforded to local organizations and socially innovative initiatives to have some social political transformative impact. This brings to light how these organizations/initiatives should focus more on their potential role in social political transformation.

2.3.2   South Bronx Unite (SBU)

In the South Bronx Unite (SBU) case, we see innovative actions by grass roots movements and organizations working to resist perceived threats (including, for instance, eviction of tenants in public housing, displacement of traditional small business, gentrification, pollution due to rising traffic congestion). They took advantage of the shifting political climate that gave rise to the Occupy! movement (in the same way that BOM took advantage of the change in urban policy at the end of the 1980s and beginning of the 1990s in Belgium, Flanders and in Europe). The trigger of SBU's major actions was a huge real estate lead project for the waterfront renewal: SBU reacted with an alternative proposal, the Mott Haven Port Morris water plan.

The SBU was enabled by a strong existing assemblage of progressive organizations in the South Bronx (many of which are now active supporters of SBU's work). It is not a particularly democratic organization in traditional terms. It uses collective leadership and changes leadership roles according to the skills that are needed to negotiate, organize actions, set up projects and so on. More information can be found on this in the book I co-wrote with Diana MacCallum, but especially in the work published by Mark Parés, who developed together with his American colleagues this case study in great detail (Parés et al. 2017; Moulaert and MacCallum 2019).

In its current incarnation, SBU provides a network node for activism and concrete avenues for connecting political with practical action. Through its advocacy planning activities, it translates political claims into community-based, environmentally just development plans, and creates possibilities for their institutional realization. SBU and its organizational partners, undertaking many and varied local projects and using social media as a self-organizing communication tool, support the development of bonding and bridging social capital, active citizenship and collective leadership around its issues of concern.

2.3.3   Anti-Eviction Movement in Barcelona

Barcelona and Catalonia are probably one of the most prominent contemporary living laboratories of how social and political worlds influence each other, and how social movements can not only become co-creators, but also catalysts, of new styles of political leadership. Originally, say in 2012, the movement 15-M had the support of some 200 small organizations, but grew very significantly thanks to mobilization initiatives (demonstrations, public forums, occupation of public spaces and squats, etc.) and materialized in over 60 Spanish cities (Moulaert and MacCallum 2019). Estimates say that between six and nine million people living in Spain were involved. The movement also triggered similar movements abroad. In Barcelona, these socio-political dynamics took a particular and encouraging development. There, the mobilization was politically effective in that the spokesperson of the Platform for Mortgage Affected People (PAH), Ada Colau, was elected Mayor of Barcelona in 2015 and re-elected four years later (Cano Hila and Pradel-Miquel 2020).

Barcelona and Catalonia have one of the richest histories of social mobilization/organization in different existential spheres, as I like to call them, ranging from agriculture, housing, proximity services, food provision, clothing provision and so on. For a long time, after the opening up to democracy in the second half of the 1970s, there was a tight relationship between social democracy (which was still socialist at the time) and platforms that united these organizations. So there was a virtuous collaboration between the political world, on the one hand, and the organizations, on the other.

As social democracy turned increasingly neoliberal and the organizations and their platforms became (and this is a Frankish term) 'institutionally lazy', they were abandoning some of their original agendas and losing a bit of their vivacity and vitality in accomplishing their objectives. So quite a bit of momentum was lost both in regard to social political dynamics (within the social democratic party) and in the movements. Then there was a period of more or less five years, between the financial crisis and 2012, in which social organizations and activists' initiatives were still active in taking care of the needs in their neighbourhoods (the Anti-Eviction movement was particularly effective) but were less effective in mobilizing politically.

2.4   Drawing some lessons from these examples

Now we should draw a few lessons from this. First off, an ecological conclusion, if you like, is that institutions and movements are linked to the natural life cycle: they are born, rise, mature and die out (Moulaert et al. 1997). Of course, institutional dynamics can be renourished—new initiatives and actors are needed for example. Second, maybe people need to suffer badly before they can be mobilized and/or come as a group of people to the streets to change a city government from a tolerant neoliberal regime to a radical, grass roots-based regime. I hope I'm not too pessimistic, but it is hard to mobilize people for change, especially when the well-off middle class acts as negationists as far as environmental threats and social exclusion are concerned; and when large parts of the deprived population have lost any perspective of socio-political change or trust in the so-called political class.

The platform for mortgage-affected people in Spain, which united numerous organizations working for re-housing (confiscating/squatting houses that were appropriated by the banks and so on), really became the basis for a very strong political movement. And what are we scientists doing there, besides being part of the action and mobilization? One of our tasks is to understand and better analyse the dynamics of governance; more research is needed on governance dynamics in planning and development. In our Planning and Development in KU Leuven, we have undertaken research (also inspired by Bob Jessop and Erik Swyngedouw's work) on different forms of governance, including hierarchical forms of governance, market-driven forms of governance, and relations of governance that are built on networking practices, more egalitarian ways and forms of governance that are based on Kropotkininan mutual aid.[4]

Now, if you take these latter forms of governance together and put them for example in a political economy, or even better (given the ecological problem we are facing now), if you put them in a political ecology framework, you can build quite a powerful dialectical theory of local governance (which is analysed as a kind of hybridization process between these different forms of governance). Then, you can start studying, for example, the life cycle of a local organization (such as GASAP), which in the beginning only had to take care of its governance but then also had to address the questions: What do we decide? How do we find enough farmers as well as land for them? How do we get our clients together? How do we build our first network of relationships between suppliers and demanders of healthy food and so on? Such an organization reaches out to other organizations that are faced with similar issues, such as having to talk to land owners to get access to more cultivable land, how to position short supply chains to holistic and monopolistic markets that are like a combination of market governance with hierarchical systems and concentration of power. Is it possible to create legally protected niches in which short supply chains can subsist and grow?

So, we need to understand the interaction between these different forms of governance in order to be able to come to an analytical conclusion on what the possibilities of bottom-linked governance are in the real world. This is where I think science can play an important role, providing scientific analysis while at the same time keeping grass roots organizations with their feet on the ground and showing them what the possibilities may be of breaking through a social political regime and entering into conflict with it, negotiating modes of governance with it and working towards a more durable, a more sustainable, socially innovative transformation. This type of approach not only provides an empirically sound analysis of how governance can be shared between civil society, the State and so on (its challenges, threats, etc.), but also returns dialectical analysis to the study of governance. This type of analysis shows the necessity of a fundamental transformation of the State and State–civil society relationships. It shows the limits of local bottom-linked governance only and the necessity of dismantling the neoliberal State, its public management governance style, its hostility towards redistribution and its budget austerity.

2.5   Conclusion

I conclude with a socio-political observation pointing to the necessity of a fundamental transformation of the State and State–civil society relationships.

I argue that you *need* local initiatives and their experiences of a new type of democracy (bottom-linked democracy), in order to work towards a durable transformation of State and civil society relationships. The Barcelona experience shows that necessity—so did the BOM and many others.

What these experiences show is that socio-political regimes make the difference. They are de facto multi-scalar. Local States can be more or less autonomous, but in many countries, State funding and control mechanisms remain at the national or supra-local level. 'Central State blackmail and sabotaging of local regime reconstruction …' is a well-known phenomenon among civil society organizations and change-prone local authorities.

The Barcelona experience shows the fragility of change processes. It has been successful in providing and implementing services at the neighbourhood level but its resources for housing policy are limited, because most of these should come from the Region or the National State. The local government led by the mayor should make a stronger case on the necessary political transformation to make these resources available. Of course, time dynamics also play a role. For example, we know from practice that if you want to change a local public transportation system, it takes time. You have to decide, you have to plan, you have to find the appropriate construction firms—you get the idea, it takes a few years to put it all in place.

Multi-scalarity in the governance system matters. Beware not to define it in a systemic approach; multi-scalarity is about scalar interactions that are socio-politically built, politically constructed, involving social political negations, electoral mechanisms, but also struggle.

I conclude by pointing out that the concrete examples of SI, territorial development and socio-political transformation we have studied provide the groundwork for seeing how social practices of citizens are essential for re-thinking our political system. Our analysis of bottom-linked governance and SI initiatives within local communities and neighbourhoods shows that though they involve struggle, conflict and varying degrees of success, they are triggers for both social and political change. As such, they represent a key for unlocking socio-political transformation that may bring us to the deep democracy we so desperately need.

Notes

1. The problematization approach was further developed and applied in SPINDUS; see Segers et al. 2016.
2. In her research, Manganelli finds that institutional governance tensions related to the co-construction of modes of governance across city divisions, community agencies and diverse food system players are the breeding grounds for, and form triggers of, co-learning in a more diverse and complex Toronto food movement world—all whilst interacting with international food policy networks.
3. Cecilia Rocha is Director of the Centre for Studies in Food Security. She was a member of the Toronto Food Policy Council and is a member of the International Panel of Experts on Sustainable Food Systems (IPES-Food).
4. On Kropotkin, see Chapter 1.

References

Cano-Hila, A.B. & Pradel-Miquel, M. (2020). Barcelona: towards new forms of institutionalising civil society and social innovation initiatives? In A.B. Pradel-Miquel & M. Cano-Hila (eds), *Social Innovation and Urban Governance*, 86–105. Edward Elgar Publishing.

Christiaens, E., Moulaert, F. & Bosmans, B. (2007). The end of social innovation in urban development strategies? The case of Antwerp and the neighbourhood development association BOM. *European Urban and Regional Studies*, 14(3), 238–251.

De Schutter, O. (2002). Europe in search of its civil society. *European Law Journal*, 8(2), 198–217.

Eizaguirre, S., Pradel-Miquel, M. & García, M. (2017). Citizenship practices and democratic governance: 'Barcelona en Comú' as an urban citizenship confluence promoting a new policy agenda. *Citizenship Studies*, 21(4), 425–439.

García, M. (2006). Citizenship practices and urban governance in European cities. *Urban Studies*, 43(4), 745–765.

García, M., Eizaguirre, S. & Pradel, M. (2015). Social innovation and creativity in cities: a socially inclusive governance approach in two peripheral spaces of Barcelona. *City, Culture and Society*, 6(4), 93–100.

Klein, J.L., Fontant, J.M., Harrisson, D. & Levesque, B. (2017). El efecto transformadorde un ciclo de innovaciones sociales en Quebec. In L.I. Gaiger, A. Mendonça dos Santos & R.S. Sao Leopoldo (eds), *Solidariedade Popular Emancipacoes*, 154–174. Editora Unisinos.

Kropotkin, P. (1914 [1902]). *Mutual Aid: A Factor of Evolution*. McClure Philips & Co.

Laino, G. (2012). *Il fuoco nel cuore e il diavolo in corpo: la partecipazione come attivazione sociale* (Vol. 39). Franco Angeli.

Manganelli, A. (2020). Realising local food policies: a comparison between Toronto and the Brussels-Capital Region's stories through the lenses of reflexivity and co-learning. *Journal of Environmental Policy & Planning*, 22(3), 366–380.

Manganelli, A. & Moulaert, F. (2018). Hybrid governance tensions fuelling self-reflexivity in alternative food networks: the case of the Brussels GASAP (solidarity purchasing groups for peasant agriculture). *Local Environment*, 23(8), 830–845.

Martinelli, F., Moulaert, F. & Novy, A. (eds) (2013). *Urban and Regional Development Trajectories in Contemporary Capitalism*. Routledge.

Moulaert, F. (2000). *Globalization and Integrated Area Development in European Cities*. Oxford University Press.

Moulaert, F., Delvainquière, J.C. & Delladetsima, P. (1997). Les rapports sociaux dans le développement local: le rôle des mouvements sociaux. In J.-L. Klein, P.-A. Tremblay & H. Dionne (eds), *Au-delà du néolibéralisme: Quel rôle pour les mouvements sociaux?*, pp. 77–97. PU Quebec.

Moulaert, F., Jessop, B. & Mehmood, A. (2016). Agency, structure, institutions, discourse (ASID) in urban and regional development. *International Journal of Urban Sciences*, 20(2), 167–187.

Moulaert, F. & MacCallum, D. (2019). *Advanced Introduction to Social Innovation*. Edward Elgar Publishing.

Moulaert, F., MacCallum, D., Van den Broeck, P. & Garcia, M. (2019). Bottom-linked governance and socially innovative political transformation. In J. Howaldt, C. Kaletka, A. Schröder & M. Zirngiebl (eds), *Atlas of Social Innovation. Second Volume: A World of New Practices*, 62–65. Signature Books.

Moulaert, F. & Mehmood, A. (2020). Towards a social innovation (SI) based epistemology in local development analysis: lessons from twenty years of EU research. *European Planning Studies*, 28(3), 434–453.

Moulaert, F., Rodríguez, A. & Swyngedouw, E. (eds) (2003). *The Globalized City: Economic Restructuring and Social Polarization in European Cities*. Oxford University Press.

Moulaert, F., Swyngedouw, E., Martinelli, F. & Gonzalez, S. (eds) (2010). *Can Neighbourhoods Save the City? Community Development and Social Innovation*. Routledge.

Oosterlynck, S., Novy, A. & Kazepov, Y. (eds) (2019). *Local Social Innovation to Combat Poverty and Exclusion: A Critical Appraisal*. Policy Press.

Parés, M., Ospina, S.M. & Subirats, J. (eds) (2017). *Social Innovation and Democratic Leadership: Communities and Social Change From Below*. Edward Elgar Publishing.

Rocha, C. (2016). Opportunities and challenges in urban food security policy: the case of Belo Horizonte, Brazil. In M. Deakin, N. Borrelli & D. Diamantini (eds), *The Governance of City Food Systems: Case Studies From Around the World*, pp. 29–40. Fondazione Feltrinelli.

Scott-Cato, M. & Hillier, J. (2010). How could we study climate-related social innovation? Applying Deleuzean philosophy to transition towns. *Environmental Politics*, 19(6), 869–887.

Segers, R., van den Broeck, P., Khan, A.Z., Moulaert, F., Schreurs, J., de Meulder, B., … & Madanipour, A. (eds) (2016). *The SPINDUS Handbook for Spatial Quality: A Relational Approach*. Academic & Science Publishers.

Swyngedouw, E. (2005). Governance innovation and the citizen: the Janus face of governance-beyond-the-state. *Urban Studies*, 42(11), 1991–2006.

3 Is Emancipatory Politicization Still Possible Today?

Erik Swyngedouw

Many of us would love to live in a different world. And a proliferating number of prefigurative social networks and initiatives around the world experiment actively with, and demonstrate practically how different socially more equitable and environmentally more sensible worlds can be created. In their extraordinary attempts to create new living arrangements and new socio-ecological relations, such initiatives demonstrate actively the astonishing transformative potential that lurks within the interstices of the existing order. It is not a surprise, therefore, that many critical social scientists and activists mobilize and foreground these innovative socio-ecological practices as markers and catalysts for a wider socio-ecological transformation. In sum, alternative or new prefigurative social practices are customarily regarded as potential foundations for inaugurating a different world. In other words, innovative social practices are deemed to constitute the basis from which to create a different and more inclusive socio-ecological order. In this reflection chapter, I shall argue that social practices in themselves—however important they may be as prefigurative examples—_do not_ change the world: political practices change the world. I shall suggest that socially innovative experimentation, although a key and vital ingredient to nurture emancipatory social change, is politically non-performative if not articulated with politicizing movements. I shall insist, therefore, that more attention needs to be given to the theoretical, intellectual and practical elements of political processes, and how these interact with and re-enforce new social forms.

This chapter focuses on the question of 'the political' and its role in galvanizing social change. 'The political' can be discerned at moments when 'the people' act in ways that disrupt the existing configuration and, in the process, constitute new forms of living and acting together. As Michel Foucault put it: 'The people are those who, refusing to be the population, disrupt the system' (Foucault 2007, p. 44). The 'political' in this context draws on the force of people who refuse to be the objects of government. In this contribution, I am neither concerned with the question of politics or of governance (although, of course, public management is important), nor with politics as it unfolds *within* the State, that is, the intricacies of its functioning at the local, regional, national or international levels. I am focusing here on the political as it appears *at a distance* from the State. The key insight is that transformative social change does not emerge primarily from inaugurating new social practices (although this matters in important ways), but from political action and organization. As French philosopher Alain Badiou put it: 'I think what is Marxist, and also Leninist, and in any case true, is the idea that any viable campaign against capitalism can only be political. There can be no economical battle against the economy' (Badiou 2001, p. 105). In other words, effective social transformation is enacted through political means rather than through innovative social practices. In sum, we need to foreground thinking 'politically' about the world, rather than 'sociologically'.

The chapter is organized in four sections. In Section 3.1, I explore Social Innovation (SI), collective experiments and political insurgencies (of the kind that Frank Moulaert presents in his reflection piece), which we see unfolding in so many places around the world. I consider these to be extremely important. They are forms of experimentation—of social experimentation and ecological innovation—that aim at prefiguring new forms of organizing collective life. Those who engage in these experiments may have a wide range of motivations and aspirations, yet cannot know a priori what the outcome may be of their actions, whether or how the experiment will work, and so on. Many fail while others are successful. But they all share a view that their experimentation is not merely for experimentation's sake: it is an attempt to prefigure a new world, to suggest that an alternative way of organizing life is possible, to show that change can happen. These are experimental prefigurations that hint at the possible making of an *other* world *in* the world. They demonstrate that a more equal, more democratic and more ecologically sane society is not only possible, but eminently practical.

In Section 3.2, I present a diagnosis of the present paradoxical situation whereby, on the one hand, while these socially innovative experiments are widespread and offer kernels of hope for change, they unfold, on the other hand, in a context that is marked by what many interlocutors refer to as an era of de-politicization and the seemingly inexorable rise of autocratic, populist and nativist regimes that seem to undermine the democratic constellation from within.

In Section 3.3, I make a case for an urban critical and political theory that moves beyond, at least in part, the critical social theory of the city that has been at the forefront of radical and emancipatory thought and practice since the early 1990s. I argue for pushing towards a more politically inflected critical theory of the urban.

I conclude in Section 3.4 with a few thoughts on how we might want to think—and conceive—of a performative radical political theory and practice for the present situation, and whether emancipatory politics are still possible in the twenty-first century. Either we believe, theoretically and practically, that a different and emancipatory politics is still possible, and act and think accordingly; or we give up on this idea, and become the social managers of a fast-forwarding twenty-first-century capitalism.

3.1   Collective experiments and political insurgencies

Since the early years of the twenty-first century, we have seen an extraor-dinary proliferation of a wide range of SI practices and of collective ecological, social and economic experiments, which Frank Moulaert and others have so eloquently written about. We have also seen a wide range of intense forms of what I and others have called 'urban political insurgencies' (see Swyngedouw 2018). These are moments of intense out-bursts of social discontent, expressed in urban uprisings that contest the inegalitarian and undemocratic configuration of the existing situation. Examples of such rebellions are the Indignados in Spain, the Outraged in Greece, the umbrella movement in Hong Kong, or similar insurrectional events discernible during the 2010s in the streets of Sao Paulo, Santiago de Chile, Istanbul and elsewhere. These uprisings of popular and mass discontent *all* share, despite unfolding in very heterogeneous geographical contexts, both a critique of the inegalitarian and non-democratic configurations that they live in and a demand for democratization and its associated institutional change.

In addition, more classic working-class movements have surged. Take, for example, the movement of the gilets jaunes wreaking havoc in French cities. They have managed to sustain their insurgency in the face of Macron's (quite extraordinary) mobilization of both discursive as well as physical violence. Or take the activist ecological movement Extinction Rebellion who mobilize direct action strategies in their call to declare a climate emergency. Another example is the high school kids joining up with Youth for Climate who walked out of their classrooms, upsetting their teachers, their parents and the ruling elites. Thousands of 15-year-old adolescents roaming the street, a bit naive, having a great day out and a lot of fun but, most importantly, demanding radical change. Some of these proliferating insurgencies demand and fight for what some would call a new constituent order: a fundamental change in institutional and governmental arrangements, of local, national and international public life. I insist that these are political interruptions of a special kind—in the sense that they unfold and erupt at a distance from the State (Abensour 2004). They neither emerge from within the cosy cocoon of participatory, consultation-based or institutionalized state-orchestrated processes, nor do they come about through public–private partnership meetings or similar forms of new governance arrangements.

Of course, instituted forms of governing do matter and are significant (as the case of Barcelona testifies), particularly in their potential synergic interaction with insurgent mobilizations. The mutual re-enforcing of mobilizations at a distance from the State and transforming institutional arrangements within the State constitute the vector through which transformative practices become both enacted and institutionalized. However, the insurgent actions mentioned above are rarely performative in terms of altering the politico-institutional configuration, and in particular, in really nudging the deepening of austerity and neoliberalism towards a more inclusive, socially and ecologically sensible way of governing. In fact, I would argue that there is an increasing gulf opening up between insurgent movements, on the one hand, and the act of governing, on the other, something that might lead to a further radicalization of insurgent activities.

3.2   A diagnosis of our times

Indeed, both socially innovative practices and politicizing urban insurgencies unfold against the backdrop of deep and pervasive processes of what some commentators have dubbed as a process of de-politicization. The latter takes the form of a deepening post-politicizing and post-democratic constellation. This refers to the increasing hegemony of consensual urban techno-managerial forms of governance, customarily supported by populist gestures that maintain that austerity-infused neoliberalization is the only possible way forward, a view generally supported by the right and the traditional left political parties. A range of authors have identified and diagnosed these consensual forms of governance as post-democratic (for a review, see Swyngedouw 2018).

One of the salient features of post-democratic forms of governing and the discursive frameworks that sustain them is the continuous invocation of a permanent state of emergency. These emergencies apparently call for immediate and far-reaching interventions; they are based on expert advice and demand specific techno-managerial remedies irrespective of popular support or endorsement. I would situate these emergencies that infuse much of the governing discourse and practice around four themes:

1. The economic-financial configuration: the imperative of sustaining the integrity of the financial-economic system has become a key task of the State at all scales, whereby a particular set of techno-managerial interventions and modes of action are proposed and implemented as the only possible way forward. In doing so, democratic procedures are suspended and assumedly unavoidable measures are implemented. The case of the Greek financial crisis and its management is a telling example.
2. International terrorism: the threat of terrorist action remains a key public concern, and prompts a wide range of surveillance, control and containment techniques. The sustained build-up of the security apparatus and the nurturing of a state of emergency puts the State on high alert. This threatens the democratic control of the State while securing the immunological desire that animates many people's libidinal attachment to the existing situation.
3. Migration: migration *is* clearly an emergency that is nurtured by a range of social and political forces. Here, too, the standard narrative is that the State will take control by erecting barriers, building camps,

and subsidizing repressive regimes like the Turkish, Lebanese and Moroccan States to keep refugees from entering Europe, leaving them to mop up the unwanted outsiders in order to protect the immunological safety spaces of the European elites.

4. The climate and ecological crisis: here, too, a narrative of pending catastrophe and galloping ecological decline feeds a dystopian fantasy that is countered by an equally phantasmagorical discourse and practice, which maintain that appropriate techno-managerial dispositives can be marshalled to contain the crisis while assuring that the hegemonic socio-ecological order can continue a while longer.

The cultivation of a permanent state of emergency suspends, or threatens to suspend, proper democratic institutional configurations at all scales. It is characterized by what Pierre Bourdieu called the 'economization of politics' (Bourdieu 2002): only those public choices that operate according to a market logic are considered to be reasonable, and can be subjected to democratic dispute. All other choices are deemed nonsensical or irrational. Despite reasonable claims that the only way in which it might be possible to deal with our ecological condition is to change the management of our common resources, to turn them from a private to a common resource, the political implications of such a stance remain disavowed. While there is widespread debate on nurturing 'the commons', the socio-legal and political implications (i.e. the requirement to dispossess the possessors and turn the common basis of life into common ownership—what would necessitate the socialization of the means of production and reproduction) remains obscenely disavowed and censored in most public debates: 'Oh, common resources are fine, but the political names of common resources we don't dare to utter!' And if you utter them, they are considered to be unreasonable or nonsensical. So, the de-politicization of the economic coincides with economizing politics (i.e. only those choices that fit on an accountant's market-based spreadsheet can be considered reasonable, while all others are deemed unreasonable) (Brown 2015).

A deep depoliticization of the economic implies that there is no longer any reasonable dispute over how to organize socially the appropriation of nature, its transformation, and the distribution of nature in the form of goods or services. There is only one institution apparently capable of doing so effectively, efficiently and equitably, and that is a more or (preferably) less regulated market. No other mode of production, distribution and reproduction is deemed reasonable, practical and equitable. Despite all manner of social experimentation (with different ways of appropriating nature, and distributing its goods), the market is consensually considered to be the only possible institution that can do so effectively, and this consensus is legitimized and deepened by the continuous mobilization of the 'right' expert voices. It is this expertocracy that insists that no other choice is possible on which the political elites legitimize their techno-managerial interventions. Moreover, the dominant discourse insists successfully that this one-dimensional perspective secures the greatest happiness and welfare for the greatest number of people.

The governance arrangements that impose the 'emergency' measure are increasingly autocratic at different geographical scales. While often legitimized by invoking public participation through public–private partnerships—and thereby bypassing instituted democratic procedures— the democratic content of such governance arrangements is highly questionable. Such forms of governance instil further a post-democratic configuration: *Who* participates in these public–private partnerships? Who is invited to participate in governing? These forms of organization are precisely the autocratic forms of governing that suspend the proper democratic forms of accountability, legitimacy and so on. As Ulrich Beck put it, these forms of governance arrangements are full of 'unauthorized actors' with unclear, fuzzy and often non-existent democratic entitlements, lines of accountability or recognized legitimacy (Beck 1997). In addition, who votes for them? Who gives them the entitlement to speak? They are unauthorized political actors. This unfolds in a context, as I have said earlier, of a generalized consensus (irrespective of one's social, geographical or gender orientation) on current key issues and problems. While there is a consensus on the issues of public concern, they need to be addressed by means of technical and managerial interventions, which are deemed to be appropriate to manage the situation without altering the foundational socio-ecological relations.

This form of consensualizing techno-managerial governance suggests, and often aspires towards, a cohesive social arrangement, one in which everyone takes part, in which everyone is apparently included. However, the reality of the situation suggests that such a post-democratic governance arrangement is not that cosy at all. While these post-democratic configurations are being constituted and deepened, there is simultaneously greater fragmentation, more intense conflict and increasing outbursts of radical discontent. These forms of discontent take two forms that cut through this attempt at consensualizing governance arrangements. One form gathers around the ethnic evil (be it ISIS and radical Islam, or white racist supremacists, like the Flemish Block 'Vlaams Blok' and part of the NVA in Belgium, or racist outbursts by all manner of ethnic groups). The other takes the form of violent urban dissensual eruptions/riots. For example, in 2006 and 2007 in France and in 2013 in the UK, urban rioters took to the streets looting shops and engaging in violent encounters with the police. These eruptions of discontent are, in many ways, politically impotent. These rioters do not always know what they want; they know, rather, what they do not want. Invariably, the elites stage them as outcasts, as not belonging, and are placed at the margin of social respectability. Remember how Nicolas Sarkozy, Minister of Interior of France at the time, called the rioters 'Racaille!' This term was verbatim repeated in London, Birmingham and Manchester by David Cameron, prime minister in 2013, using the English translation, 'Scum!' When the riots were over, the left leaning Social Democratic (Labour) Council of Manchester, pasted advertisement slogans on local trucks, depicting brooms with the slogan 'Let's sweep the city clean.' It is not difficult to discern the double meaning captured by the slogan: both the rubble and the 'scum' had to be swept from the city streets. The word scum or racaille, in ancient Greek, is *ochlos* (rabble), which referred to those who were not properly constituted as citizens of the polis (i.e. the *demos*, the name of the people as a political category) and who were not part of the demos—the ochlos were the scum.

Besides this visible and very urban eruption of discontent, we find a third expression of discontent, one in which 'the political' can be discerned. These revolts embody and express what Alain Badiou calls the return of the passion for the real under the banner of equality (Badiou 2012). By the 'real', he means a passion for the emancipatory, egalitarian, political transformation, as manifested by political insurgencies such as the Spanish Indignados, the Occupy! movement or Black Lives Matter. These are uprisings that elites have responded to by saying, 'Oh, they are not political. In fact, those who rise up do not know what they want.' That's what Bill Clinton said to the Occupy! movement in Wall Street: 'You guys and girls do not know what you want.' To which some of the Occupy! people cleverly responded, 'You cannot give us what we want.' *That* is the political statement.

As already mentioned, I suggest that these movements are often impotent, politically speaking. They are like a jelly pudding: they shake things up for a brief moment in time to then return to 'normal'. Protesters return home, to their job, their family, their schools; one cannot occupy places on a permanent basis.

Most participants in such urban rebellions often act in what Jacques Lacan would define as 'hysterical': while 'tickling' and 'questioning' the dominant master-narrative, they in fact further solidify the hold of the Master over the discursive and policy field. While revelling in the fantasy of engaging in a political act, usually very little in terms of institutional or socio-ecological change happens. Nonetheless, their politicizing potential should not be underestimated. Let me illustrate this. First, the 2013 Davos World Risk Report (written by the managers of planetary urbanization, the 'Master planners of the earth', who are primarily concerned with making their dreams for the world geographically materialize) identifies the great obstacles that stand in the way of the implementation of their dreams for the world. In the report, they consider 'the rise of seeds of dystopia' (the proliferating urban rebellions). This suggests that these insurgencies *did* shake the feathers of the assorted leaders of the world a bit. They were concerned about the rise of global anti-capitalist discontent. Second, and as discussed by Frank Moulaert (pp. 53–54), the quite radical transformation of Barcelona's governance was directly articulated with the 15-M movement and the close articulation between political movements and urban rebellion. Third, the spectacular (albeit short-lived) success of SYRIZA in Greece who formed a radical left government was elected for the first time on the wave of the popular anti-austerity revolts. These vignettes suggest that political insurgencies *do* have an identifiable political performativity.

3.3   Foregrounding critical political theory and practice

I argue, therefore, for a greater theoretical and practical attention to be paid to the urban political configurations of the kind I mentioned above. I do this for a number of reasons.

First, since the early 1990s, critical theory has become predominantly social critique, largely ignoring the insights from critical or radical political theory and practice. While the plurality of social power relations along class, gender, sexual or ethnic inscriptions has been thoroughly examined, attention to emancipatory political transformation waned. The horizon of the possible seemed to be sutured by focusing on various modes of resistance to existing power relations rather than considering strategies and possibilities for transgressing the entrenched inegalitarian order. Indeed, the overwhelming emphasis since the early 2010s on social and ecological movements have led to a marginalization and silencing of politicizing processes of emancipatory transformation. The celebration of 'resistance' trumped concerns with the political dynamics necessary to produce a more egalitarian, solidarity-based, and ecological sensible world in the world.

In critical urban scholarship, we have been preoccupied with urban social movements, of a variety of kinds, which we strangely and too easily identified as political agents. From the 1980s onwards, ever since Manuel Castells' seminal *The City and the Grassroots* (Castells 1983), urban social movements have been a narrow lens through which we have articulated urban politics and urban strategies. In doing so, we have strangely conflated social processes with political ones, and thereby neglected taking 'the political' seriously as a theoretical and practical terrain. We have argued that the *social* is the terrain for enacting socio-ecological transformation. There has been an unsubstantiated presumption of a close relationship between critical social analysis and emancipatory political practice. And it is precisely this close relationship that requires close scrutiny. There has been a too easy presumption of a direct relationship between social practices, innovative or otherwise, and political transformation. Nonetheless, as Alain Badiou suggested polemically, there is no direct or causal connection between social analysis and transformative politics.

There is an urgent need, therefore, to rethink urban politics and urban political theories and practices in ways that are more sensitive to considering the city as the site for political encounters, political interruption and political experimentation. The urban has indeed always been the site for the performative staging of social and political equality, for experimenting with the making of new forms of democratization, and for nurturing radical imaginaries of what 'urban democratic being in common' might be all about. This involves no longer focusing exclusively or predominantly on institutional politics, institutionalized politics or urban social movements, but also on considering other forms of contestation and disruption (even though they may lack organizational form, legitimacy, or clearly legible and institutionalized forms of social organization). The focus of theoretical and practical attention needs to move to considering the emergent practices and imminent manifestations of explicitly *politicizing* urban gatherings that aim at transforming both the institutional order and the existing governance arrangements.

3.4   Conclusion: what to think?

The political implication of the argument unfolded above nurtures a view that foregrounds insurgent urban democratic acting, one that operates at a distance from the State and aims at transforming the instituted forms. To put it simply, if one wants to change the world, this has to start from the streets, from public space. These forms of insurgent urban acting are always specific, concrete and particular, but the specific and concrete grievances are turned into a universalizing demand for inclusion on an equal base for all manners of people (irrespective of their gender, religion, skin colour or belief systems). These practices also operate through the production of their own spatiality; these are insurgent planners at work. They produce literally their own geographies: geographies of encounter and of meeting, combined with the physical infrastructures that go with these.

In concluding, I present a number of questions for us to think about. First, how can we articulate (if it is still possible), these particular, specific geographically situated interruptions? Second, can processes of emancipatory universalization that are radically inclusive still be thought and practised? How can we move from an emphasis on resistance and critique (that is, a negative dialectic of critique) to a positive dialectic of transformation that answers the question of 'What is it we want?' While we excel at expressing 'What do we not want?', it seems much harder to symbolize in political terms what is it we *do* want. What is the name we give to such a political project? What is it—or what could it be—if we refused to do what we are told to do? What does it mean to think through the disconnectivity, if indeed that is the case, between social theory and political practice? What does it mean to define emancipatory politics as 'radical equality that nurtures diversity in different situations'? Can we still demand what the dominant order considers to be impossible—but what we know is eminently possible? How can we prefigure new democratic practices in an agonistic space? How do we do that? How do we plan for that? How can we mobilize again what Cornelius Castoriadis and others call the 'radical imaginary' (Castoriadis 1994)? Has it not always been the very staple of planning to imagine the impossible, and make it happen somehow? Should we not first and foremost traverse the fantasy of the elites—the fantasy of the consensual order, the fantasy that says, 'Yes, times are troubled; yes there are problems in our cities, in our regions, in our ecologies. But don't worry we have the right techno-managerial means to deal with these. Your future is in safe hands.' That's what they promise, but it's a fantasy. The elites insist that the catastrophe is imminent if their recipes are not followed. Should we not muster the courage to tell them 'It is already too late: the catastrophe has already happened, not for you or for me, but for most people who are already too poor, too hungry, too sick and too disrespected to act. They live in ecologies that are unsustainable, they live in a catastrophe every day.' If we were to argue that the catastrophe is not something yet to come, but that it is currently in place (combined and uneven), how would we then begin to deal with our urban social and ecological issues? What do we propose if we were to give up on the fantasy of the elites?

References

Abensour, M. (2004). *Democracy against the State.* Polity Press.

Badiou, A. (2001). *Ethics – An Essay on the Understanding of Evil.* Verso.

Badiou, A. (2012). *The Rebirth of History: Times of Riots and Uprisings.* Verso.

Beck, U. (1997). *The Reinvention of Politics: Rethinking Modernity in the Global Social Order.* Polity Press.

Bourdieu, P. (2002). Against the policy of depoliticization. *Studies in Political Economy,* 69(1), 31–41.

Brown, W. (2015). *Undoing the Demos – Neoliberalism's Stealth Revolution.* MIT Press.

Castells, M. (1983). *The City and the Grassroots: A Cross-Cultural Theory of Urban Social Movements.* University of California Press.

Castoriadis, C. (1994). Radical imagination and the social instituting imaginary. In G. Robinson & J.F. Rundell (eds), *Rethinking Imagination: Culture and Creativity,* 136–154. Routledge.

Foucault, M. (2007). *Territory, Population: Lectures at the Collège de France 1977–1978*. Palgrave Macmillan.
Swyngedouw, E. (2018). *Promises of the Political: Insurgent Cities in a Post-Political Environment*. MIT Press.

4　Exploring the Dilemma between Self-emancipation and Self-responsibilization

Bob Jessop

In this Dialogue book, Frank Moulaert and Erik Swyngedouw's reflection pieces engage in what I would call 'parallel play' rather than interactive play. I see my job as connecting the two and, as such, my reflection piece serves as a framework to situate our debate. In my view, Frank Moulaert is very much a pessimist and Erik Swyngedouw is very hopeful (if only we can learn to scream to resist, to refuse, to disengage from father State). I begin by presenting the enlightenment social imaginary of capitalism, State and civil society; I show the tensions that this entails and discuss how we can fit the idea of social movements and transformation within it. I refer not only to Foucault (which Erik Swyngedouw also mentions in Chapter 3) but also to Gramsci. Together, their work provides a good way to reflect on the challenges of social transformation and Social Innovation (SI). Then, drawing in part on Frank Moulaert's work on SI, I stress the importance of reading the conjuncture to see what might be possible in terms of a strategic defensive but tactical offensive approach. In other words, in order to promote SI, we have to know the limits of any particular conjuncture (to see how far the conjuncture may be pushed). I then introduce the idea of governing complexity, emphasizing in particular two modes of governance: network and solidarity. If we want to mobilize social movements for socio-political transformation, we must rely on networks and solidarity rather than on markets and hierarchy (or command).

One of the fundamental dilemmas of promoting SI relates to bottom-led versus top-down perspectives. From a top-down perspective, civil society and SI are in fact forms of self-responsibilization. In other words, the State and the market offload problems they can't solve saying, 'Please pick up the pieces yourself, be responsible, handle this.' This contrasts with the notion of a bottom-led perspective whereby civil society and SI are forms of self-emancipation. I address this dilemma and conclude by providing a long-term horizon to guide and frame a strategic and tactical promotion of SI.

4.1   The enlightenment social imaginary

The 'enlightenment social imaginary' emerged in Europe in the seventeenth and eighteenth centuries and reflected the far-reaching social changes occurring in this period. It has become a very conventional way of thinking about societal relations that still survives today. However, it is not how I as a critical political economist would describe society.

Figure 4.1 shows the potential tension between three main areas identified in this social imaginary, mainly that of capitalism, the State and civil society. These can be considered in terms of their role in valorization and in terms of their role in promoting social use-values. (1) In terms of capitalism and civil society (as C.B Macpherson says in his 1962 book on Enlightenment political theory), the relationship is one of possessive individualism: individual consumers/individual citizens compete to maximize their revenues. On the flip side, civil society can be a source of social values, solidarity and resistance to the logic of capital. (2) In terms of the State and capitalism, the State promotes valorization by securing the conditions for profitable accumulation. More substantively, the State also has a role in the care economy, in reproduction and in generating revenues that can be turned into benefits for civil society. (3) In terms of the State and civil society, individualized, competitive citizenship fragments individuals into so many citizens competing for their particular interests within the logic of a national interest. Alternatively, and on the substantive side, mass parties/social movements try to resist the logic of this triangle.

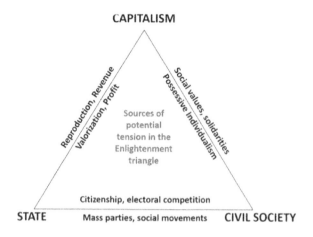

Source: Jessop 2020.

Figure 4.1   Enlightenment social imaginary

How does civil society fit into this? More recent discourses around civil society highlight the pluralist self-organization of civil society. Can this compensate for market and State failure in order to sustain the neoliberal project in the current conjuncture? Can it resist the colonization by the State or the encroachment of market forces and promote self-emancipation? At stake here is the tension between self-responsibilization and a pluralist, more solidaristic, self-emancipation project.

4.2   The state and civil society as sites of political representation: a Gramscian reading

Here I turn to Gramsci (who I'd say is 'the Marxist you can take home to mother because he is friendly and adaptable'). His concept of the State is quite different from the concept of the State in the enlightenment model of State/civil society/capitalism. In defining the State as 'lo Stato integrale' in its inclusive sense, Gramsci includes elements that refer back to the notion of civil society: 'the State equals political society + civil society'. In other words, it is 'hegemony protected by the armour of coercion' (Gramsci 1971, p. 263; 1975, Q6 §88 pp. 763–764). He then says that it is

> The entire complex of practical and theoretical activities with which the ruling class not only justifies and maintains its dominance, but manages to win the consent of those over whom it rules. (Gramsci 1971, p. 244; 1975, Q15 §10 p. 1765)

In his reflection piece, Erik Swyngedouw describes some of the mechanisms of the *entire* complex of practical and theoretical activities with which the ruling class maintains its rule. I suggest (as Erik Swyngedouw also does) that this is not how the subaltern classes approach the State because they tend to maintain a fetishistic separation between the economic and the political. He refers to the economization of economic struggle that traps it inside the logic of the economy and to the locking of political struggle inside the logic of the political. From a Gramscian perspective, political society corresponds to the direct domination exercised by the dominant group via the State and juridical government (the rule of law, police and military action and so on). Conversely, civil society is an ensemble of organizations, commonly called private (although they also remain part of the State), that is a site of political and social contestation as the dominant classes, their parties and intellectuals, seek to hegemonize it. Equally, civil society, by virtue of its private juridical political character and its separation from the public juridico-political State apparatus, can also be a source of resistance to economic exploitation and political domination. It is the sphere in which some hegemonic and counter-hegemonic projects are formed.

Frank Moulaert's work on SI and social enterprise indicates the potential of civil society to develop variations of sub-hegemonic or counter-hegemonic projects. These contest, within the limits of the possible, the rule of capital and/or the power of the State. This form of resistance is particularly important for subaltern groups and old and new social movements—that, I argue later on, draw on networks and solidarity to resist market forces and the power of government.

Another point that Gramsci makes is the contrast between East and West. When we are talking about social movements and SI, we are oriented towards the West (but as Erik Swyngedouw points out in his reflection, the West is becoming a bit more like the East). Gramsci argued that in the East, the State was everything and civil society was primordial and gelatinous; in the West, there was a proper relation between State and civil society. When the State tottered, a sturdy structure of civil society was immediately revealed: the State was just a forward trench behind which stood a succession of sturdy fortresses and employment (Gramsci 1971, p. 238). Erik Swyngedouw's reflection brings to light how far that proper relation is being undermined by the rise of an increasingly authoritarian State: one that mobilizes xenophobia, populism and so forth in order to push down and repress free mobilization of bottom-up (or bottom-led) society.

Source: Wikipedia 2021.

Figure 4.2   The storming of the Winter Palace

Figure 4.2 is an image of the storming of the Winter Palace, which was sufficient to bring the Bolsheviks to power. After their coup d'état, they engaged in a war of position to consolidate their hegemony. The opposite strategy is required within the framework of Western society, particularly after the 1870s when the masses enter the political system. As such, the struggle for hegemony is crucial.

For Gramsci, a war of position is the phase of slow, hidden conflict, where forces seek to gain decisive influence and power in society. It involves a struggle to win bases of self-organized class power, to create a socialist vision in the working class, and so to build a counter-hegemony for the socialist movement. A war of manoeuvre is the phase of direct and open clashes between classes—not just an eventual violent confrontation between the State and revolutionary forces. A war of position is the decisive struggle, even though it occurs before the open struggle that would be settled by force in a final military confrontation.

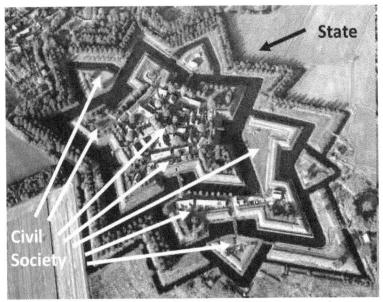

Source: https://en-academic.com/pictures/enwiki/70/Fortbourtange.jpg, amended by Jessop.

Figure 4.3   Metaphor of State as a fortress

If you think of the State as a fortress, as shown in Figure 4.3, then the State can be considered the outer casing. Where is civil society? It is all over the place, as a source of resistance. To see how this works, take for example the military coup against Erdoğan in Turkey—which was resisted through a sturdy succession of fortresses and emplacements. The military coup was supported in part by the State. But what Erdoğan did successfully (less successfully in the more recent election), was to mobilize at least half of civil society against the coup d'état. I describe this as civil society in the shadow of the State. An alternative way of thinking of this would be civil society against capital and the State. Erik Swyngedouw also provides examples of this—mostly of civil society mobilizing against the logic of the market and the logic of the State and in favour of solidarity and horizontal networking (rather than private–public partnerships, hierarchically organized).

So, how then might we understand the State and civil society as sites of political representation? Here I argue that access to the State is crucial in politics and policy. The question is whether that access to the State is within the logic of the State, or (the way Erik Swyngedouw presents it in his reflection) whether it draws from different sources. As presented by Nicos Poulantzas, the struggles outside the framework of the State force those in charge of the State (the 'State managers') to calculate what the consequences—the social and political repercussions—may be of ignoring the counter-hegemonic movements (the sub-hegemonic movements, the mobilizations of Occupy!, and so forth and so on) (Poulantzas 1973, pp. 81–85, 91–92, 97–98, 107–108).

What is the art of the possible when civil society is mobilized through solidarity and networks? In essence, this completely transforms the logic of politics as 'the art of the possible'. This is particularly important because of the mediatization of politics, and the role of the official media, social media and so on, in shaping our reality. Just look at the Donald Trump campaign in 2016 or the Brexit election to see to what extent social media can be mobilized to fundamentally shift messages and, more specifically, to influence the outcome of elections. The messaging associated with Cambridge Analytica in Britain is a case in point. Nonetheless, we need to explore the ways in which subaltern groups can use sub- and counter-hegemonic media to mobilize people. It is very important that we move beyond clicktivism where you click and sign a petition and think that somehow you are transforming the world—you are not, you are just reinforcing the power of media groups.

Here I come back to the Gramscian idea that the State is the ensemble of activities, theoretical and practical, with which the ruling class maintains its rule through active consent. This idea links up with Erik Swyngedouw's arguments about the economization of economic struggle and the parliamentarization (if I may put it in those terms) of political struggle. There is an institutional separation—a fetishized institutional separation—between the economic and political in a functioning liberal, capitalist democracy. Why? Because economic struggles occur within the logic of the free market. In other words, workers can engage in a struggle (over wages, hours, working conditions, prices, social wages, etc.), until their mobilization of economic struggles threatens the profitability of their particular firm, or threatens the profitability of the larger economy; at this point, they engage in concession bargaining—they agree to a cut in their wages, their pensions and so forth, in order to keep their job. Political struggle occurs within the logic of the representative State, based on the rule of law. In other words, individual citizens, not classes, are represented. The individual citizens are mobilized in the name of many different identities: Northerners, Southerners, Catholics, Protestants, Leavers, Remainers, Tax Payers, Welfare Beneficiaries, and so forth. Gramsci's analysis sees this as a competition around the meaning of the national interest—on how to reconcile the particular interest of citizens and property owners in an illusory general interest.

In a liberal bourgeois democracy, the dominant class must fight for political power on formally equal terms as those of subaltern classes. It is substantively very unequal. Furthermore, while the ruling classes expect workers and subaltern groups to struggle economically in economic terms, and politically in parliamentary terms, they couldn't care less about this distinction themselves. It's only the subaltern classes that fetishistically maintain the idea that the economic struggle is one thing and the political struggle is another. This, I think, is one of the hidden advantages, or perhaps now not so hidden, of the ruling classes. They see the terrain they are struggling on as being 'political society + civil society'. In order to maintain this, they are willing to engage in all matter of tactics and strategies.

4.2.1 Modes of Representation

Here I am not interested in discussing all modes of representation (Table 4.1); rather, I want to discuss pluralism—which could also be seen as the terrain of civil society. Pluralism refers to institutionalized access to the State by voluntary and legitimate social forces that represent interests, and/or causes, rooted in civil society. This involves typical forces, old and new social movements, based on diverse identities, and never one singular, strategic, essentialist line of division. This contrasts with the *Communist Manifesto*'s claim that the history of all hither to existing societies is the history of class struggle and that 1848 presented a choice of siding with the proletariat or capital. The manifesto was a particular intervention in a supposedly revolutionary moment to polarize choices for people. Very rarely are the choices presented to people put in such stark political terms. Normally they are much more pluralistic, ambiguous and ambivalent—which is one of the ways that the rule of capital is maintained, because the opposing forces are so divided and fragmented.

The crises occur when social movements are, in Gramsci's terms, decapitated. Of course, this is not a literal removal of heads; it refers to when the leaders of political parties, trade unions, or social movements are recruited and seduced by the warm, seductive embrace of the State. A crisis can also occur when compromise is rejected in a stage of immobilization, leading to a catastrophic equilibrium.

Foucault's notion of 'a dispositive' is useful at this point in my reflection. We are talking about a problem-oriented, strategically selective ensemble (or assemblage) that involves an apparatus that is decentred—comprising institutions, organizations and networks. This ensemble provides a shared strategic purpose and orientation: a discursive framework that reduces societal complexity in an emergency or a crisis by offering a simplified social imaginary to address particular problems. In order to engage in decisive action, the problem must be simplified and made manageable for it to be addressed in policy terms (requiring a particular framing and the setting up of a particular objective and intervention that captures a specific focus).

Let's take the example of the financial crisis (which Erik Swyngedouw also brings up in his reflections). The problem addressed was: 'How do we rescue the banks?' rather than 'How do we rescue mortgage holders?' It cost far more money to bail out the banks then it would have to halve the mortgage debt of all mortgagees. But rescuing the banks was in the national interest, whereas bailing out mortgage holders by halving their mortgaged debts divides property owners without a mortgage from those in negative equity—which poses challenges because of competition (the individualization of citizens). We see here, from a top-down perspective, how diverse devices and technologies are used to produce power, knowledge and problems. The elites frame the problem in ways that require it to be solved on behalf of capital and the State. They reproduce the knowledge that justifies those particular forms and interventions, and you produce the subjects that will act in line with these objectives. This represents what I mean regarding self-responsibilization: 'Oh gosh, the State is failing, the market is failing, you have to help us—as responsible citizens, as activated citizens.' This kind of subjectivity is not one that emerges bottom-up (unless it is to be seduced and captured)—the elites are framing a par-

Table 4.1   Modes of representation

Mode	Basis	Typical forms	Crises
Clientelism	Patron–client relations based on exchange of favours for support	Cadre parties run by notables, patronage parties, machines	Inability to provide flow of material concessions; social fragmentation
Corporatism	Socially designated role, task, or function in the economic division of labour. Formal equivalence	Corporativism, tripartism, soviets, council communism	Pseudo-representation, factionalism, declining fit with economic order
Pluralism	Institutionalized access to State for voluntary and 'legitimate' social forces that represent interests and/or causes rooted in civil society	Old and new social movements based on diverse identities, interests, issues, and social causes	Passive revolutions that decapitate or absorb social movements, immobilism, rejecting compromise, catastrophic equilibrium
Parliamentarism	Indirect participation of *formally* equal 'citizens' in policymaking via voting rights	Political parties oriented to territorial mobilization	Functional decline of parties, representational and legitimacy crises
Raison d'Etat	Formal representation suspended due to 'threats' to State, society, vital interests	Vested interests in the 'deep State' or exceptional parties	Dissolution of State cohesion, legitimacy, internal contradictions

Source: Jessop 2015.

ticular notion of the big society, or civil society, and so forth. This brings up the importance of conjunctural analysis, which allows one to read the conjuncture to know what is possible in a specific context.

4.2.2   Modes of Governance

In broad terms, governance is a means to coordinate complex social relations. Governance theory usually deals with the market, command and networks. I add to this list solidarity, which is crucial for understanding how we might think about SI (Table 4.2). The anarchy of exchange, the hierarchy of command, reflexive networks (horizontally networked, not vertically networked) and solidarity of unconditional loyalty and trust, rarely exist in pure form. Frank Moulaert talks of hybrid forms of governance in his reflections—of which there are many (Chapter 2: p. 48). If we want to introduce Foucault here, we can see these modes of governance as diagrams of power: matrices in and through which power is exercised and mobilized with specific effects. Though I cannot go into full detail here, within these four modes of governance (exchange, command, network and solidarity) it's the relationship between network and solidarity that I would describe as the heterarchy of civil society (or, drawing on Frank Moulaert's reflections, the basis of bottom-linked governance).

A network is reflexive and procedural; it operates through open networks and aims to produce negotiated consent rather than impose top-down views. It runs the risk of becoming a talking shop. Anybody following the Brexit debates in Britain sees what happens when talking just becomes pointless—a way of surviving day to day without reaching any conclusions at all and producing distorted communication. Solidarity is unreflexively value-oriented: 'I identify with you, I feel for you, I share your pain. Of course, I am going to support you.' Solidarity is based on commitments; the ideal type would be requited love and the opposite is betrayal (one's trust is exploited and one is left in the lurch when it is in the other's interest to leave). Solidarity should be based on unconditional commitment, the danger being that it produces co-dependency. Taking an example from family therapy, some therapists say, 'This couple is pathologically co-dependant; they would be far better separate but somehow they are getting some positive vibes by being together even though it is hurting one or both of them.' The co-dependent partner enables the bad behaviour of the selfish partner as a source of misjudged self-esteem and feelings of self-worth. In contrast, networks should generate positive gains for each participant based on solidarity that builds long-term mutuality of sacrifice. Long-term asymmetric sacrifice would be like co-dependency. When networks and solidarity work well, the basis is established for bottom-linked governance that can resist the hierarchy of command and the anarchy of exchange.

Table 4.3 presents just two dimensions of hybrid governance (discussed in Frank Moulaert's reflection piece). Here we can begin to see that the primacy of solidarity linked to exchange gives you trade unions, syndicalism, cooperatives. The primacy of dialogue, secondary role of solidarity, gives us social movements and civil society. Social enterprises, social economy, would be important for revenue generation but based on solidarity as well. This exercise can be pursued in three dimensions as well, if one had the time and energy to do so.

What are the favourable conditions for successful governance? There is a need for simplifying models and practices that are 'fit for purpose' as a basis for 'going on in the world'. Gramsci talks about the world of difference between an historically organic ideology that is necessary to a given structure and one that is arbitrary, rationalistic and willed (Gramsci 1971,

Table 4.2   Four modes of governance

	Exhange	Command	Network	Solidarity
Rationality	Formal and procedural	Substantive and goal-oriented	Reflexive and procedural	Unreflexive and value-oriented
Key medium	Money	Coercion	Meaning	Commitment
Ideal type	Derivatives	Sovereign State	Open network	Requited love
Criterion of success	Efficient allocation	Effective goal attainment	*Negotiated consent*	*Unconditional commitment*
Main sign of failure	Inefficiency	Ineffectiveness	'Talking shop'	Betrayal
Other failings	Market inadequacies	Bureaucratism, corruption	Distorted communication	Co-dependency; asymmetry
Significance	Anarchy	Hierarchy	*Heterarchy of Civil Society? Bottom-Linked Governance?*	

Source: Jessop 2020.

Table 4.3   Two-dimensional hybridity

	Primacy of Profitability	Primacy of Command	Primacy of Dialogue	Primacy of Solidarity
Secondary role of exchange	n.a.	Mafias, New Public Management	Benchmarking, Good Governance	Trade Unions, Syndicalism
Secondary role of command	Firms, Mixed Economy	n.a.	Public–private partnerships, Deliberative democracy	Bund, Commune, Associational democracy
Secondary role of dialogue	Guanxi, Network Economy	Parties, Soft Law, Cooperative State	n.a.	Community, Communitarianism
Secondary role of solidarity	Social enterprises, Cooperatives, Social Economy	Commune, Subsidiarity	Social movements, Civil Society	n.a.

Source: Jessop 2020.

pp. 377–378). The former addresses real problems and might lead to a counter-hegemonic, or sub-hegemonic dispositive.

Like Erik Swyngedouw, one of my favourite pieces of reading every year in January for the past 14 years has been the Davos report. I read them in conjunction with the OXFAM reports on inequality; I get my students to look at both every year and to follow a theme (to see, for example, how each reports the water crisis). Unlike Erik Swyngedouw, the reason I think this is important is that, if you want to know what (in Gramscian terms) an organic counter-hegemonic movement would be, you might address the problems that the leaders (the masters of the universe) see as the big problems at the moment. For Davos, now, the biggest problem is the environmental crisis. If you don't have an imaginary that addresses the environmental crisis, then you've got problems. Another hot topic is the increasing inequality of wealth and income that is delegitimizing the market, the State and so forth. If you want to develop a broad counter-hegemonic movement, address the problems that Davos worries about. That's what is going to destabilize them and make them a bit more nervous. If only you can identify or mobilize around the problems that also worry those at Davos, and not give them an answer that solves the problem in a way that they would welcome (but that solves the problem in a bottom-linked manner) then you are at least half way to winning the ideological, ideational battle.

4.3 Responses to governance failure

I have a theory—perhaps because I am a contrarian—that every mode of governance fails: markets fail, States fail, networks fail, and so does solidarity. In this section, I move on to how one responds to these failures in different ways.

Regarding governance failure, when dialogue fails, one re-orders the networks and brings new participants into the discourse. One changes the terms of the discourse, re-sets their focus on different problems to resolve. One reorganizes the conditions of self-organization (there can be a major role of the State here, such as encouraging new participants, providing side payments, encouraging trade union organization if trade unions are getting too weak, recognizing that some groups are too powerful so that one tries to intervene and tax the new social media giants and so forth, to give more space for the 'popular' voice). One creates new forms of dialogue and, in relation to solidarity, one develops new identities and encourages the shift from old to new social movements (because they are more relevant to real problems of today). In other words, a new civil society (or from a self-responsibilization viewpoint, a 'big' society) is developed.

This leads us to Frank Moulaert's notion of bottom-linked governance. 'The people are those who, refusing to be the population, disrupt the system' (Foucault 2007, p. 44). Here, the people, who are organized in their new social movements, constitute themselves as a force that strives for self-emancipation through networks and solidarity. Conversely, from the viewpoint of the system that seeks to displace the effect of market and State failure in capitalist societies, the aim is to mobilize the population to become self-responsible. This is precisely the site of the dilemmas in civil society: between self-emancipation and self-responsibilization.

Civil society can be studied as the site of strategic and tactical contestation between these different polar tendencies (self-emancipation and

Table 4.4   Paradigms of Social Innovation

	Technocratic	Democratic
Knowledge construction	Expert	Community
Effects	De-politicizing	Politicizing
Power distribution	Vertical	Horizontal
Neoliberalism	Supports	Opposes
Role in political struggle	Self-responsibilization	Self-emancipation

Source: Rows 1–4 based on Montgomery (2016, pp. 1982–1983); row 5 – own interpretation.

self-responsibilization). Above all, this means that those who are organizing as the people for self-emancipation have to resist the lure and charm of the State and the market to enter it on their terms, in the ways that fetishistically separate economic and political struggle.

Table 4.4 shows an interesting typology of forms of SI (Montgomery 2016) as being either technocratic or democratic (or, if you like, of being either self-responsibilizing or self-emancipating). Social innovation as technocratic takes the form of knowledge construction as expert, top-down and delivered (in terms of Foucault's notion of truth-regimes) to the population. It is de-politicizing, as Erik Swyngedouw brings up in his reflection: 'We know the truth, don't worry, we will solve the problem for you' (Chapter 3, p. 71). In this sense, the distribution of power is vertical, and it serves to support neoliberalism. Its strategies are flanking and supporting mechanisms that serve to keep the neoliberal show on the road in the face of its growing failures.

We can contrast this with democratic SI. Self-emancipating knowledge is constructed through self-reflexive knowledge construction/information sharing by the community. It has the effect of politicizing struggles, turning the population into a potentially self-emancipating people. Power distribution is more horizontal, based on the idea of treating each other as equals and learning from each other. Self-emancipating knowledge is opposed to neoliberalism, rather than working to flank and support it.

Figure 4.4 shows various interpretations of this knowledge paradigm. Give someone a fish and they will eat for a day; teach someone to fish, and they can feed themselves until the water is too contaminated (or the shoreline is seized for development). We can supplement this by noting that they could also feed themselves until they follow the World Banks' advice that 'shrimp fishing is really profitable so get rid of the mangrove swamps to enable shrimp farming', which means that the next tsunami may destroy the whole village. Or, if social forces support a social movement, then whatever the challenge, it can organize with its peers and stand up for their changing collective interests. This form of self-emancipation can be contrasted with supporting big society as the expansion of self-responsibilization, which David Cameron calls 'community empowerment' and Barack Obama calls 'community organizing'. What Cameron and Obama are doing is providing self-responsibilizing movements to flank and support neoliberalism to keep the show on the road.

Source: Why Hunger 2015.

Figure 4.4   Social Innovation for self-emancipation

I suggest that we think about how one might understand self-emancipation through networks and solidarity. What I mean is opposing the principles of neoliberalism (i.e. liberalization promoting free market competition). Self-emancipation should as far as possible limit free market competition, not favour monopolies but promote social enterprise and social surplus generation (not profit generation). Rather than supporting deregulation, it should support empowerment—enhancing the role of the people by linking direct and representative democracy. It should also oppose privatization and support socialization—expanding the social economy focused on social use-value rather than exchange-value. It should not favour as much free trade as possible, but fair trade. This involves re-directing taxes (there will still be taxes, this depends on your view of how things might be financed) as well as citizen wages and car allowances. It also requires new forms of distribution, universal public services and a redesigned State in order to support the bottom-linked governance mechanisms.

4.4   Looking ahead

I now explore the question of how we can reorganize the economy in order to enhance exchange-value (or should we be thinking more of social-value?). We can define production in Polanyian terms (but also perhaps Marxist terms) as the expenditure of labour-power (human creativity and energy applied to material and symbolic provisioning) and creation of (potential) use-values. Capitalism is universalized commodity production: all inputs taking the form of commodities (including labour power, land, money, knowledge) and all use-values are produced for sale, hence having (potential) exchange-value. There is a tension between organizing production around use-value and organizing production around exchange-value. This creates a series of tensions, contradictions and dilemmas around the relation of use-value and exchange-value. And missing from this simple presentation is the question of how 'social values' mediate the relation between use-value and exchange-value.

Building on the Marxist notion that political economy is a political economy of time, I suggest that the only time that we are free is in our free time. This means that the development of a social economy (the orientation of SI and so forth) should be first and foremost oriented to the maximization of free time, rather than necessary time (which is subordinate to the logic of competition, valorization and so on).

Figure 4.5 shows my image of society in terms of the enlightenment trinity that we are living in at the moment (in terms of capitalism, civil society and State). The dominant sphere is profit-producing production and reproduction in capitalist social formations. There is also a non-profit-producing production and reproduction sector; feminists will talk of unpaid domestic labour, and there are many other forms of unpaid caring labour and self-care (like the allotments created in guerrilla gardening). In a situation dominated by capital accumulation, there is always a risk that the non-profit-producing production and reproduction sector is really subsumed under the logic of capital accumulation; it becomes a sphere of self-responsibilization rather than self-emancipation. Equally, in the opposite direction, it can be a powerful source of resistance, which one wants to see expanded. The non-profit sector doesn't exclude exploitation or oppression (as any feminist critic of unpaid domestic labour will say, it is the site of paid and unpaid labour, paid for by taxation or socialization with a major contradiction where you are trying to reduce the cost of labour power by exploiting the non-profit sector). However, capital wants to reduce the size of that sector, because it's not generating profits through commodification, commercialization and so forth. So, the key question is: Can we reduce social and necessary not-for-profit labour time to free up time for profit-producing labour?

The area of free time for (solidaristic) self-realization is the area within which Marx would consider we are free: the area of free time for self-realization. Either it is a marginal mode of living (showing that another world is possible) or it risks capitalist colonization. We then have to think of many activities that we used to do for fun, like running or cycling, and look to see to what extent they are now also sites of capital accumulation. You need the latest running shoes, you need this brand-new carbon fibre bike frame, or whatever. The gym: you no longer go for runs in nature, but you need to go to the gym and be subject to the logic of self-improvement and so forth. The non-profit-producing sector can operate thanks to the inputs of solidarity, or it can become parasitically exploited.

Figure 4.6 presents an image of the long-term horizon using the same basic model. Note that the weight of the different spheres has changed:

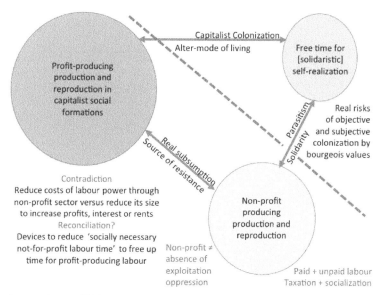

Source: Jessop 2019.

Figure 4.5   The current capitalist social formation

profit-producing production and reproduction, in socialist societies, has a minimal role but it provides inputs for the non-profit-producing production and reproduction centre. It is regulated to limit rents, suffers taxation to secure revenues for the non-profit sector and, as a key factor in socialist societies, involves social enterprises, cooperatives and so forth that are producing outputs to move into the non-profit-production and reproduction centre, which are based on mutual respect (with no exploitation or oppression). Governments prioritize solidarity and networks, basic income, care commons, universal basic services, socialization tightly coupled with free time, solidaristic for self-realization. New subjectivities change the ways in which those in charge of social enterprises, the social economy, see their goals. Now it's oriented towards social values (rather than exchange-values); just as you get market inputs into the big non-profit sector, social values also enter into that sector—they are tightly coupled. The line of division is not, as seen earlier between these loosely coupled sectors versus free time; now, the logic is to link these sectors

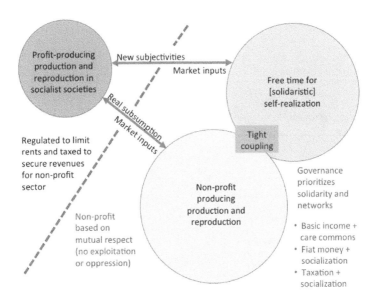

Source: Jessop 2019.

Figure 4.6   Long-term horizon for self-emancipation

together tightly, and provide a minimal role for a profit-oriented (or rather revenue-oriented) sector.

4.5   Conclusion

What does all this mean for bottom-linked governance? What are the conditions for bottom-linked governance to work well? In any complex system, one needs requisite variety for flexibility. One must maintain a repertoire of forms of governance suited to different kinds of objects and goals. One also needs to continually monitor progress against the declared social objectives: being willing to recognize things are going wrong and being prepared to recalibrate and rebalance the forms of governance. Finally, one needs romantic public irony. To quote Gramsci, this involves pessimism of the intellect, optimism of the will. Why is it public and romantic? Because, as I have said, everything fails; and as such my long-term horizon is going to fail as well. If everything fails, one can't choose to succeed, but one can choose how to fail. If one is going to choose how to fail, one should choose how to fail wisely. What's the wisest way to fail? By failing together, through participation and dialogue, through networks and solidarity. The irony is that by choosing to fail, by mobilizing networks, solidarity, reflexive solidarity and so forth, you are reducing the risk of failure. This is a different way to interpret pessimism of the intellect, optimism of the will. 'If graffiti changed anything it would be illegal' (Banksy)—but that also applies to social media, if they are mobilized for self-emancipation and resist self-responsibilization. Do not resist purely through graffiti, do not resist purely through clicktivism; we must engage in bottom-linked mobilization. These conclusions are my attempt to synthesize two papers and add my half pence of sociological or governance theoretical, of Gramscian or Foucauldian wisdom. Let us now engage in the debate.

References

Foucault, M. (2007). *Territory, Population: Lectures at the Collège de France 1977—1978*. Palgrave Macmillan.

Gramsci, A. (1971). *Selections from the Prison Notebooks*. Lawrence & Wishart.

Gramsci, A. (1975). *Quaderni del Carcere*, 4 volumes. Giulio Einaudi Editore.

Jessop, B. (2015). *The State: Past, Present, Future*. Polity.

Jessop, B. (2019). Kapitalismus, Staat, Transformation: Neosozialismus oder demokratische Ökosozialismus? In K. Dörre and C. Schickert (eds), *Neue Sozialismus: Solidarität, Demokratie und Ökologie vs. Kapitalismus*, 97–110. Oekom.

Jessop, B. (2020). *Putting Civil Society in its Place*. Policy Press.

Macpherson, C.B. (1962). *The Political Theory of Possessive Individualism: From Hobbes to Locke*. Clarendon Press.

Montgomery, T. (2016). Are social innovation paradigms incommensurable? *Voluntas: International Journal of Voluntary and Nonprofit Organizations*, 27, 1979–2000.

Poulantzas, N. (1973). *Political Power and Social Classes*. New Left Books.

Why Hunger (2015). Global movements program: supporting movements for food sovereignty and agroecology. 23 April. https://whyhunger.org/category/articles/global-movements-program-supporting-movements-for-food-sovereignty-and-agroecology/.

Wikipedia (2021). The storming of the Winter Palace. https://en.wikipedia.org/wiki/The_Storming_of_the_Winter_Palace.

5   Debate: A Dialogical Encounter on the Potentialities of Social Innovation for Social Political Transformation

The reflection chapters of this book (Chapters 2–4) were presented as lectures preceding a debate held at the Department of Architecture, Faculty of Engineering Sciences, KU Leuven, on 4 April 2019.[1] This chapter provides a written rendition of the debate, which was organized in a question/answer format from the audience but also involved a free-flowing conversation between the three speakers.

The debate brings to life the tensions, differences and confluences of the three thinkers' approaches to analysing the potential of new forms of social engagement in bringing about socio-political transformation in a socio-ecologically inclusive and emancipatory way.

The questions from the audience first cover a range of issues, centring mainly on the 'ingredients' needed to provoke the desired change, given a context where people no longer believe in the political. Though no set recipe exists, the speakers explore how exactly the politicization of social movements occurs and what needs to happen for people to invest themselves fully in reinventing the political. The discussion takes into account the rise of post-truth/post-politics/post-democracy, and what this says about the current state of affairs (i.e. how do we explain the rise of right-wing supremacist movements?) and of current emancipatory initiatives. The debate is propelled forward by the implications of these analyses, discussing what social movements say about the future of the political and politics and touching on everyone's personal responsibilities vis-à-vis this current state of affairs.

5.1   On integrating time and space in social innovation analysis

Audience: Can you say that bottom-linked governance can avoid (what Erik Swyngedouw speaks of as) technocratic de-politicizing answers, or (as Bob Jessop would say) can it avoid just serving the reproduction and accumulation of capital? And to Bob Jessop: Does your framework take into account territorial disparities and how can this also be addressed? How do you integrate time and space into your analysis?

Frank Moulaert

Bottom-linked governance is realized, constructed and deconstructed within time dynamics, and I'm glad that Bob Jessop refers to conjunctures and conjunctural moments. It is obvious that in Antwerp, for 10 to 15 years, these socially innovative dynamics (that gave a highly prominent role for bottom-linked governance) only lasted as long as there was a political regime whose agents were interacting in a positive way with these initiatives. And that could lead to a very fundamental criticism of the approach I'm using, saying, 'Well, if the social political regime does not follow, then your initiatives will peter out.' But that was not my message. My message was that the dynamics seeding into bottom-linked governance practices are not just an experiment of building socially innovative initiatives, and are not just building a mode of interaction and communication with local governments, but are also an experiment towards *transforming* the working of local governance (recognizing of course that State dynamics do not stop at the level of local government). At the same time, I make the observation that local government cannot function if it doesn't interact with the other levels of governance and if it does not enter into conflict with other levels of governance. So place matters, yes, because in our way of analysing space/time dynamics, we recognize places that are, at a certain point or epoch in history, much more open to social political change or places that are much more resistant or much more constrained to socio-political change. But at the same time, it is *only* through the social political dynamics at interactive spatial scales that you will in the end (together with the other forces I'm not delving into now—I leave that to Bob Jessop to do) lead to the social political transformation we need. Take, for example, the big movement of the social economy that started in the second half of the nineteenth century: it was a long-lasting movement with different conjunctural moments that in the end led to a very creative confluence of scientific practice nourished by economic, social and political theory and mobilization (in terms of social movements and politics). I'm not implying that what we are witnessing now will lead, in the next few years, to a drastic social political transformation. But I'm convinced that—as argued in my reflection piece (Chapter 2)—bottom-linked socially innovative experiences are part of a wide movement that can lead to social political transformation. These include experimentation, new learning dynamics (on how democracy should work in society and in the polity we dream of), a bold proliferation of movements and mobilization. Erik Swyngedouw, Bob Jessop and I all provide examples of what is possible and of what could grow and evolve towards the social political transformation we hope for.

Erik Swyngedouw

One of the big challenges (theoretically and practically) today is that local political events that I describe in my reflection piece (insurgencies that erupt as imminent to the situation) are rarely translated into politicized movements (Barcelona being an exception). On the whole, what we see today is political events that, as Badiou would say, are characterized by three things: (1) they are localized: they always emerge within a specific localized environment; (2) they are extremely intense: involving a very intense 'full-time' process, which is not sustainable in the long term; and (3) they rarely translate in a politicizing procedure that ends in institutional change and transformation. In other words, they rarely translate into a sustained politicized process of change. It is also important to note that the participants in these events are socially heterogeneous: men and women, workers and intellectuals and all sorts of new social agents.

We do know how politicized procedures unfolded historically. If you go back to the nineteenth or twentieth century, it is clear how a political event would turn into an emancipatory sequence: these were centred on a privileged subject (the proletariat, i.e. the agent who would *do* it), it had a particular form of organization (the political party—be it socialist or communist), which would be fighting to occupy the State. It produced the welfare State—an extremely significant, although imperfect, emancipatory social transformation. Most people today in the twenty-first century would argue that these three key elements in processes of politicization do not work anymore. The proletariat as the preferred political subject is questionable; the hierarchically organized political party as the key organizational form is as dead as a donkey; and occupying the State is not any longer sufficient in a time of generalized globalization.

I think the examples of Barcelona or Greece and a few others are interesting because they experiment with new ways of bringing together different social subjects into a unified form of political subjectivation, where women and men hold hands and experiment with new performative organizational forms and with new tactics of occupying power. But none of the three things I mentioned above (privileged political subject, organizational form, and necessary site[s] for political occupation), at this moment, are very clear, especially in terms of considering what might work and what might not work politically. The latter refers of course to the modalities through which sustainable and emancipatory institutional change is achieved.

The key question, therefore, is: how do you trigger and sustain a politicizing sequence? Take the issue of water privatization in Barcelona (whereby the municipality seeks to municipalize the privately organized water system). It is very interesting to see how the debate is being framed: the elites do everything they can to turn the issue into a techno-managerial one, irrespective of whether water delivery is publicly or privately owned. Some of those more politically inclined say, 'That is not our issue. We're not concerned primarily with the technical and managerial structure of the water company, we are interested in the political ideological question as to whether nature should be commonly owned or privately owned.' So these are the sorts of mechanisms through which a politicizing sequence can be sustained; and *that* is what is failing at this moment. There is no shortage of bottom-linked practices, but these do not easily universalize out—and *that* is what is required for sustained politicization.

Of course, most attempts at emancipatory politicization are resisted: take the example of Turkey. What is happening right now (Erdoğan's nationalist-autocratic populism) cannot be understood without understanding the events that unfolded in Istanbul in 2013 in Gezi Park. Erdoğan's State authoritarianism was a direct response to the threat that was signalled by the success of Gezi Park; Erdoğan was very good at preventing the politicization of this process. A similar process can be discerned after the Arab Spring or SYRIZA's success in Greece. The elite's resistance to forms of emancipatory politicization is indeed profound and often violent, thereby thwarting any attempt at inaugurating a political procedure. These forms of systematic mobilization of real or discursive violence from the part of the dominant social forces are rarely explicitly recognized or taken into account. It is imperative, therefore, to *dare* to stare in the face the violence that parallels politicized struggles. For example, the financial and political elites mobilized all manner of tactics to curtail SYRIZA's progressive politicization in Greece. They go to great lengths to ensure that a movement does not shift from a localized uprising to a universalizing procedure. When a social movement has a chance of success, the elites' hammer comes down hard—it comes down with extreme violence. If we cannot formulate an adequate answer on how to deal with mobilized violence at moments that politicization succeeds, then we will find it very difficult to deploy effective political strategies for lasting political change.

Frank Moulaert

I think your historical reading of the building of the democratic system (the parliamentary system) is biased. The social economy movement to which I was referring earlier, for example, and which we could say went parallel to the democratization process, was as important for the democratization process and for the building of the democratic State as the political struggle. So if you make this analysis and want to transfer your analysis of the role of the social economy to the contemporary times, you have to take seriously what's going on in these social movements (and in their mobilization processes) and you have to take seriously their political significance. You said that there is a mushrooming of initiatives, and that there is a lack of mobilization between these initiatives (networking between these initiatives), and especially of political translation of these initiatives. I doubt that. Political mobilization has a different meaning today—we're living in different times: the proletariat is no longer the majority of the population; the population that is suffering is composed of very diverse groups. And here comes in Frank Moulaert's pessimism: Barcelona probably works because tens of thousands of people were living in the street, because privatization was so deeply felt that the only possibility to work politically was through the social organizations, because these social organizations *were* taking care of the needs of the people.

To conclude my thought with a question (I leave the word to Bob Jessop now): have you given up on the State as an arena for class struggle or not?

Bob Jessop

How do I integrate time and space into my analysis? I think the positive examples that are being given are very time- and space-specific. If I look at the British State, it is incredibly centralized. Over the last 20 years, the ability of local governments (city governments and so forth) to take initiatives has been marginalized. There has been cut after cut after cut: local authorities have been forced to privatize everything, just to enable them to continue with current expenditure. And the ability of a Barcelona or your other examples where social innovation, social economy, social enterprise are working and working well, is in part because they're being supported in one way or another by a local State and by a large part of the population who brought the new local political leaders into power. If I look to see where in the United Kingdom, we are seeing Social Innovation—it is very much bottom-linked, but often not much linked to the State. It's grass-roots mobilization, mobilizing voluntary services and so forth as a form of self-emancipation. A very good example, in a period of austerity, is the development of food banks. That is a *real* bottom-up initiative, where there is a little bit of support from church or philanthropic organizations but little from the government (perhaps it may provide a town hall where the food bank operates but is not particularly favourable towards it). And Jacob Rees-Mogg, the ultra-Brexiteer is on record saying, 'The problem is if you offer food banks, people will take advantage of them. There's no real demand. But if somebody offers you free food, you'll go for it.' Critics can't even comprehend that it might be necessary for people to go to a food bank because they're telling an entirely different story. But, in reality, millions of people in Europe depend on food banks for their survival.[2]

So I think that the first thing that matters is that you have to take into account the structures of the State: whether or not the State can act in the way that Frank Moulaert thinks it can and Erik Swyngedouw perhaps thinks it can't is irrelevant—the structures of the State constrain opportunities for local authorities and local initiatives.

Poulantzas offers three ways of thinking about the State in his *State, Power, Socialism* (1978)[3]: there are struggles to *design* the State, there are struggles *within* the State and there are struggles *at a distance* from the State. Redesigning the State is absolutely fundamental to enabling SI to occur and that should be an important part of any social innovation, social economy, bottom-linked strategy. In other words, you need to redesign the State to enable it to support these initiatives. There may or may not be struggles within the State, over whether we should support it or not, but then the mobilization outside the State (which Erik Swyngedouw talks a great deal about) is also crucial. Frank Moulaert does as well in his own vocabulary. So, this is where the place/space dimension takes place. I think there's a problem if you fetishize place, because there is a real problem of parochialism against which this already relatively rich country through social innovation protects itself, insulates itself, even more from the logic of globalization, environmental catastrophe and so forth. I think therefore, that this notion of horizontal linkages has to look beyond a particular locality, beyond a particular region, beyond a particular nation, in order then to transfer best practice, etc. Best practice not in the sense of one size fits all, but to share experiences. And I think this is one of the benefits of Frank Moulaert's initiatives (lots of different little local case studies, lots of different local lessons, lots of networking initiatives).

There's a nice distinction introduced by Michel de Certeau between strategy and tactics. He says the bourgeoisie has strategy (it has war of position); it's much more difficult for subaltern classes to use this, and they have to resort to tactics (which is the mobilization of time that Erik Swyngedouw speaks of): interruptions like the gilets jaunes, specific interventions, and mobilizations that have an impact. But if they're not careful, they dissipate and become overnight wonders (15-minute wonders and so forth). And the problem, then, is to connect those tactics back to Gramsci's war of position.

5.2 On social innovation and political or governance forms

Audience: Is Social Innovation only possible within democracies? In other words, is democracy a precondition/prerequisite for SI? If not, how can SI happen in countries with other political or governance forms?

Frank Moulaert

Socially innovative initiatives happen in a particular societal context. And there is no a priori necessity to say that it should be in a democracy, or in another social political regime. Good socially innovative practice has as an ambition to realize bottom-linked governance, and also includes strategies meant to put it in place. Bottom-linked governance is not a static relationship with the local State; it has as an ambition to make the local State more responsible (in a way similar to that by which the needs of the people are activated in the social movements of the social initiative). This relationship is conflictual and involves learning between both parties, and indirectly learning together how democracy can be reinvented. In saying this, I imply that bottom-linked governance is in a way essential for new political movements and for re-politicizing society. It's not a question of what comes first.

Most of the experiences we looked at happened in a democratic context, but these democratic systems work in very different ways. Take Belgium: you can say that Belgium has a well-working democratic system, but if we were to bring Belgians' opinion on their democracy together, we would end up with a picture of a very handicapped democracy. The idea that building democracy is one thing and doing socially innovative initiatives is another thing is a dualistic dangerous way of thinking; for me the two are very strongly related. I'm not saying that socially innovative initiatives and the building of bottom-linked governance will ultimately lead to a better democratic system. I'm saying that it is an important ingredient of strategy or vision of how we can work towards better working democracy (meaning one which takes into account all the essential needs of its citizens).

Bob Jessop

Gramsci drew a distinction between East and West, where in the East the State is everything, and civil society is weak and gelatinous. And I think whether we're looking at the Soviet bloc, or military dictatorships and so forth, we're looking at situations where civil society is weak and gelatinous. What that means is not that there's no solidarity, but that solidarity is very tight knit (within a particular family, ethnic or faith network); you wouldn't extend that trust or solidarity to a whole society (let alone beyond it). Even in the most authoritarian regimes, networks continue to operate as one of the ways in which people survive (i.e. without informal networks and solidarities it would be impossible to survive on a day-to-day basis in an authoritarian or totalitarian regime). What that means is that there is social innovation going on (not in the emancipatory sense that Frank

Moulaert would want to talk about but in the sense of self-survival) but that it is incredibly constrained by the structures of political power.

Erik Swyngedouw

In response to Frank Moulaert, I agree that no political transformation is possible without experimental innovative social practices. It is like a Chesterfield sofa, where the knots hold together the tapestry; the knots are the forms of experimentation, but the tapestry is also needed.

The process of emancipation that is articulated through social practices (on the one hand), and political practices (on the other hand) is very different and mutually reinforcing. Most social, ecological and social innovative projects are dealing with questions of equality and unfold in a context of frustration and of disempowerment (a context of real, sometimes perceived, inequalities). Social initiatives try to validate and transform these existing (well-understood and analysed) inequalities. The political strategy is centrally about universalizing or spatializing these practices that are prefigured through socially innovative experiments and practices.

Frank Moulaert

There's a big similarity with what was going on in the cooperatives and the first unions (building solidarity between each other)—this was an important element in the building of democracy as of the nineteenth century.

Erik Swyngedouw

I agree with that. However, the difference is that political democratization is predicated on the *assumption* of equality: it *presumes* that we are all equal (in a context where we all [empirically] know that that is not true). So, there are different notions of equality at work: social equality (or social inequality that can be addressed or countered through social practices) versus democratization, which insists on the presumption of equality of each and all qua speaking beings. The tension between these notions of equality needs to be continuously 'kept alive', so to speak. In other words, a clear conceptual and practical distinction needs to be maintained between the sociological notion and practice of equality, on the one hand,

and political equality, on the other. The first is predicated upon identifying, socially speaking, the mechanisms of inequality and engaging in strategies to transform the process in egalitarian directions, while political equality is predicated on the axiomatic assumption of principled equality of each and all irrespective of their social and bodily inscriptions. The articulation between these two notions of equality is of the utmost importance in any emancipatory project.

On civil society and State interaction. The emancipatory process is that which produces equality and freedom. By freedom, I am not speaking of freedom as 'the freedom of choice' (that is a liberal notion), but as the capacity to do what you *have* to do (not what you *choose* to do) because you have no other choice. While (neo-)liberal notions of equality revolved around the liberty to choose from what is on offer, emancipatory freedom is predicated upon doing what one feels as an utmost necessity, what one feels one has to do. These notions of equality and freedom have to be historically continuously re-constituted, they have to be invented and reinvented.

Let's take the example of gender equality. If you were to say, in the eighteenth century, that there is a fundamental equality between men and women, no one would understand. It took more than a century to actually begin to symbolize, organize and discuss questions of gender equality, and to give some sociological content to the issue. What does it mean to be gender equal? When the feminist movement started to be politically performative, in the late nineteenth and early twentieth centuries, it emerged on the basis of the axiomatic principle of equality, and it would take more than a century to symbolize, express and institutionalize the social substance and practice of gender equality. It is only now that we are *beginning* to find an answer to the question of what constitutes gender equality. Do we have a final answer? No, we don't. So, the very notion of emancipation is never fixed: it's continuously reinvented and redefined, and new forms of equality/inequality keep on being foregrounded. As such, I agree with Bob Jessop that every attempt at emancipation fails, and has to fail, meaning that we should try harder and fail better next time. And that, of course, takes a gamble. And this is what I think most people are extremely afraid of—of acting without knowing what the outcome is going to be. In fact, we have to act knowing that the outcome will be different to what we might imagine or expect it to be. So, let's not be afraid of failure because fail we will: and only then can we hope for some form of political transformation.

Frank Moulaert

I agree with Erik Swyngedouw. The building of democracy, as we know it, has been a very long process that was full of failures *both* in political terms and in terms of social economic experiments (the building of cultural circles, building of educational circles, etc.). So, I make a plea: you cannot make an analysis of a politicization process without looking at the connections between all these different movements and initiatives and by recognizing the political meaning therein. I think you are overdoing it by stressing that 'this is political, and this is not political'. I mean, if we build democratically governed research laboratories and groups, I think we're experimenting a social as well as a political practice.

5.3   On civil society and reinventing the political

Audience: If we see that the need for civil society often arises in a certain zeitgeist (which is I think something you all three agree on), then how do we design a more structural system that allows for this continuously changing civil society to continuously form a new political platform? And if the answer is to some extent to tie civil society more locally, do we then not lose all of our duties in tackling larger societal issues? (Because if we attempt to tie down more civil societies to a more local level, do we doom ourselves to not discuss things like climate change or societal issues as a civil society?)

Bob Jessop

This to me is the wrong question: you're asking for a top-down design that guarantees the ability to people to self-emancipate. This is a contradiction in terms: to think that somewhere, there is some 'metagovernor' in the sky that can come up with the perfect constitutional, institutional, juridical, political, economic design (a 'meta-Davos' of sorts! If this existed, I would certainly claim that on my own initiative in the future!). Rather, what is essential is to create space for a strong, pluralistic and heterogeneous civil society to debate and be self-reflexive in order to understand and practise what's working well and what isn't working well (requisite variety). In other words, there needs to be a lot of flexibility inscribed within the governance system. Anybody who thinks that it is possible to come up with a design that fits everything for all time for any particular locality is telling you a fairy story: I call this 'unicorn thinking', miraculous and magical thinking. What's important is to create the space for people to learn from their (collective) experiences, correct their mistakes, to comment on different activities and move forward.

Audience: Regarding Erik Swyngedouw's presentation: many policymakers are yearning to find consensus—the argument is that this would lead to peace. Could you elaborate on how consensus politics can lead to violent eruptions?

Erik Swyngedouw

The State, whatever form it takes, tends or at least pretends to speak for the whole society (with the exception of an authoritarian State). What I call a post-political/post-democratic consensual arrangement refers to that which is nominally democratic in the sense that different views are invited and incorporated within an overall consensual techno-managerial configuration. Those who are excluded from this consensual arrangement are the radical outsiders: those who, despite the attempt at consensus, are systematically excluded from the consensual order.

So, the flip side of a consensual polity (that claims to include all) *always* has an excessive remainder. In other words, any instituted order is always predicated upon selective exclusion (like migrants, or Jews, or women, …). The classic example of this 'remainder' are those who feel, on their bodies, that austerity is systematically excluding them from full participation in life; or, of course, the undocumented immigrants (the ones who do not have a voice, who cannot be included). It is precisely through these excessive remainders that ruptures, fragmentations and outbursts of discontent and disagreement (of either violent or nonviolent character) occur. In other words, the eruptions of discontent are almost without exception animated by systematic outsiders (to what is presented by the elite as a consensual arrangement). So, the basic point is that consensus, by definition, always fails in a neoliberal class-based, gender-based configuration: the systematic outsider *cannot* be included. And it is precisely *this* that opens up the necessity for re-politicization. ('I do not count! I am going to make it count!') From this perspective, any consensualizing order is doomed to fail as its attempts to cover up tensions and conflicts that will inevitably return at some point as forms of contestation and overt conflict.

Frank Moulaert

At the same time 'I do not count! I am going to make it count!' is the trigger for many social innovative initiatives.

Bob Jessop

I get to be piggy in the middle again! I agree with what Frank Moulaert said, but I'd rephrase it in Marxist and Gramscian terms. Civil society, the economy, the polity—are based, essentially, on a heterogeneous set of particular interests. And as Rousseau pointed out, you cannot turn the 'will of all' (of every single particular interest against every other particular interest) into the general will. I drew on a Marxist notion, also taken up by Gramsci, that the consensus is always a representation of an *illusory* general interest. What that means is that there's always a set of insiders whose particular interests are privileged and an excluded group whose particular interests are largely marginalized (the undocumented migrant is a very good example; during the period of the post-war, with the welfare consensus, it was the disabled, women, immigrants who were not part of the consensus system, which was dominated by the white male breadwinner). This reflected the strategic importance of the white male breadwinner in the Fordist accumulation regime and electoral system. And what that means is that the illusory general interest is *always* going to fail, because there are always particular interests (sometimes just one, sometimes a large number) that get excluded. Sooner or later, any particular State, acting in the name of a particular illusory genuine interest, is going to see the contradictions and the failures increase. This then leads to the re-politicization of what was previously a sedimented/taken-for-granted uncontested illusory general interest. And that's when you get the scream, the cry, the excluded demanding entry and so forth. And that's where social movements become important because they start to speak on behalf of not just a particular interest, but *sets* of marginalized interests. And that's their strength and their potential: they don't just contest saying, 'We're being left out'; they say, 'We share a lot in common with other people who are being left out.' And that's the basis then for the mobilization of social initiatives of many kinds.

Frank Moulaert

Yes, that's when we try out new forms of democracy.

Bob Jessop

Yes. And I think the history of the rise of democracy is a very good example. It wasn't just workers organized into trade unions; it was workers putting savings *into* building societies to generate the money to be able to start buying or building a house, or contributing to funds for funeral societies (in mutual insurance funds), or creating friendly societies (where somebody is going to be sick, and there's no State welfare as yet). So, the rise of democracy isn't just 'we want the franchise'. It is drawing on a whole series of networks and solidarities that show that we have a lot in common (not merely in our wage-earner role, but in our wider membership of civil society). I think one of the real risks now is the increasing Statization, or commodification, of so many sites in civil society that diminish the wide-ranging capacity evolved over time of the connected networks and solidarities.

5.4   On the origins of subversive initiatives

Audience: You all say that these innovative social practices need to go further, to change the social political order beyond space? Every time you mention Barcelona, it feels like an alignment of the planets (it happens once in a millennium). The implication is that the rest of Europe (especially the north) is not in dire enough straits to mobilize, create political action, and subvert the system. My question is twofold. (1) Where should we look to find initiatives and people actually willing to engage in this kind of subversion nowadays in this type of Europe? (2) When we look at politically subversive initiatives, should we only count on the marginalized population or also try to engage the people that are better off?

Frank Moulaert

First of all, I would like to qualify a little bit what you said about Barcelona: what I point out in my reflection piece is that it was also a cyclical movement. After the return to democracy, there was a strong cohesion between the social and political movements in Barcelona. This cohesion also developed into a tight collaboration with the Social Democratic Party, which lasted for several decades and, in a way, affected the vitality of the social/political movements. To simplify and exaggerate a bit, these movements gave up fighting because they could obtain what they wanted by working within representative democracy. With the financial crisis, this entente between social democracy and social movements broke up, and the social movements had to return to their old fighting spirit (rediscovering their *raison d'être* and having to respond to different needs compared to the ones that prevailed under the Franco regime, and many more social needs linked to the financial crisis). Yet what we see is the translation of the social movements into new types of political organizations, which ended up in the creation of the political party United Barcelona (bringing the anti-eviction movement to power, and led to some new forms of democratic decision-making providing a good example of a bottom-linked governance).

Now, coming to your question, I have no answer (I call on Bob Jessop and Erik Swyngedouw to answer). It is my strong intuition (and don't misunderstand me) that the proletarian environments, or a situation of very advanced exploitation or alienation (socially, politically, economically) is a much more fertile ground to stir social political movement that can lead to social political transformation. As to the role of the bourgeoisie? In many historical movements, bourgeois intellectuals played a very important role as leaders, but they counted on the social political power of a large number of people who were in a very deprived situation.

Bob Jessop

Okay, I think I'm going to disagree with Frank Moulaert for a change, regarding the relationship between economic transformation and political transformation. If I understood you correctly, you were saying that the more subaltern groups are immiserated, left behind, or proletarianized, the more likely they are to become politicized. That was one of the views that Gramsci strongly criticized: that all we need to do is to wait for the economic crisis to intensify, and then the workers will spontaneously rise up on the basis of syndicalism. The Italian communist leader, Amadea Bordiga, was an example of a politician taking this economistic position. In other words, the worse the economic conditions become, the better the prospects for revolution.

I think this is where Erik Swyngedouw's point about the primacy of the political is absolutely crucial: you need to also put in place the conditions for political mobilization that go beyond those who are left behind. So, let me give you a counter-example. What do we know about the groups that supported Donald Trump? It was the white working class, the white supremacists, who felt really left behind. What do we know about the groups where the highest concentrations of Brexit leave votes were? They were stronger among the most immiserated, the most left behind, the poorest localities, the ones that had suffered the most cuts in terms of austerity; it was the biggest decline since 2010 (in the UK case, in terms of economic growth). Just waiting for conditions to get worse doesn't necessarily lead to left-wing SI-oriented mobilization.

Frank Moulaert

I didn't say that.

Bob Jessop

I know. But what I'm trying to do is to point out that we need to think about social bases of innovation in more than class terms. And I take this point a little bit further: if what we mean by the proletariat is manual workers (skilled or unskilled) in manufacturing industry, then all the figures in Europe show that (with only two exceptions in two countries) they would never have been the majority. You have to mobilize far more than the proletariat in the strict sense. You need to look to develop cross-class alliances. And I've always thought that one of the strengths of the social innovation approach is that it's not tied to a particular class identity, but it draws on a heterogeneous set of social identities, with projects that look beyond how one might reorganize the economy—it is emancipatory in that sense. And, so, I want to think about the social bases of social innovation in terms of the left behind or the marginal/subaltern and not in a narrowly, almost technological, Marxist sense. And I agree, that's not what you're saying. But I want to point out the danger of looking to immiseration as the route to mobilization: in doing so, you run a whole series of risks seeing the rise of xenophobia, white supremacism, right-wing populism (the kind that Erik Swyngedouw was talking about) in these terms. I think that the strength of the SI approach is, in fact, going beyond a narrow interpretation of the economic basis of social innovation and towards forms of solidarity and network (of the kinds where people identify with others than those in their particular occupation). Though this is not what you said, it is a risk presented if you start thinking in those terms.

Frank Moulaert

I take your point very seriously. But this brings me to things Erik Swyngedouw says in his reflection piece. Rewording Erik Swyngedouw's point in my own terms and using consumerism as an example: as long as we can shop, we won't participate in political mobilization. In my language: socially innovative initiatives mobilize people, but this is not enough—it is not enough, not necessarily because the mobilization has no political meaning, but because the numbers are simply insufficient. How do we increase these numbers? Can you answer that Erik Swyngedouw?

And the second thing is the role of false truth (referring to Bob Jessop's examples of Trump voters). False truth is not new of course; fascism used false truth through other media (they used physical public space instead of public social media to sell false truth).

Erik Swyngedouw

There is no strict correlation between the social position one has and political subjectivation. In other words, anyone can become a political subject. Most don't. Bob Jessop quotes Gramsci several times (and this is very rarely taken seriously) 'the pessimism of intellect, the optimism of the will'. You have got to *want* it! You have got to *WANT* it! Most people just don't want this kind of transformation. And here I include *us* in the first place (and here I come to the numbers issue). As I said in my reflection piece, there is no shortage of people who do all sorts of things, who mobilize and engage in all manner of social and political projects. I do think, however, that many of the present-day liberal intellectuals (like most of us in this auditorium) are part of the problem. So, who's my adversary? Who am I talking to here? It's *you*. That is, the liberals—these are, for me, the problem. That is, the absence of political subjectivation of the majority of liberals today (certainly in the global North). We accuse our enemies of being the problem (what does my enemy do?), but rarely examine reflexively our own position as liberal intellectuals. The problem is the liberals who profess that they want to change, who are politically aware of the multiple power relationships etc. that lead to the condition in which many people find themselves, who profess to the need of building progressive movements, ... but who at the end of the day, *do jack shit*.

So, I think today's key problem is not the *absence* of politicizing activists or politicizing social innovative projects. The problem is we liberals who refuse to join up with them, and always critique the situation. So I am very much on Slavoj Žižek's side when he says that the key problem today is the fact that we know very well what the situation is (ecologically, socially, in terms of capitalism, exploitation, etc.) but we act out our everyday lives as if we do not know. That holds true for us in the first place. It's our refusal to speak, to take the jump, to take the gamble of becoming political subjects. That is part of the problem.

Frank Moulaert

What would you have to change in your behaviour?

Erik Swyngedouw

I don't know, exactly. Not flying around, for example? There are all sorts of things. In a nutshell, what I invite you to do, and what I'm trying to do myself is to *think* again. A radical transformation of thought is required in order to align our thought and intellectual practice with the actual politicizing forces that are working towards making a new world in the world.

The key question is: What to think? What to read? And what to say? There is an urgent task, therefore, to go back to the library, and read Gramsci, read Marx, read the nineteenth-century Social Innovation literature. And start thinking again rather than repeating age-old analyses and perspectives. We need to have more faith in our own capacity to *think*. That is the most revolutionary act today: that is to say, 'I don't care about my next publication, I'm going to go to the library and spend the next six months reading the three volumes of *Das Kapital*.'

Bob Jessop

If I can just reinforce the point with reference to Marx and Gramsci. In *The German Ideology* (which is a critique not of the German ideology, but a critique of German intellectuals), Marx and Engels write that the trouble with intellectuals is that they spend all their time thinking about ideas. This leads them to think that if you change ideas, you change the world. And *that* is exactly what they are critiquing: the inability of ivory tower intellectuals (or those that spend all their time reading, writing and talking to fellow intellectuals, students, etc.) to have any transformative impact at all. In order to bring about transformation in Gramsci's terms, we need to become organic intellectuals engaged with the social innovation movement (social enterprise movements, etc.) and learn from them—not just from the books that we read, the latest fashions etc.

[Applause]

In that sense, just engaging in critique is to fall exactly into the trap that Marx, Engels and Gramsci are warning us against—that is, we become purely disembodied, disconnected intellectuals. Until we link up with real social movements and learn from them as well as provide them with insights that go beyond their particular experiences, we're just going to reproduce the de-politicized set of social movements.

5.5 On triggers of political mobilization

Audience: You are telling us that we—the liberal European masses who are privileged enough to listen to you right now—should think and act differently. Again, what is the trigger to move this mass of liberals if it's not material need or social exclusion? Is it only about personal ethics?

Bob Jessop

Whether it's personal ethics, I don't know. But it certainly requires a sense of solidarity with those that are suffering, and not to just live off the privileges of being (in our case) well-paid white male intellectuals in relatively neat institutions.

Erik Swyngedouw

I fully, *fully*, agree with you. Take the example of the gilets jaunes: I keep on reading analysis after analysis by critical scholars (usually sociologists) who say, 'masses of people with clear views, particular demands and with communist elements within it …' And I say 'Yay, that's precisely what we need!' What are the intellectual articulations that I can make with the gilets jaunes movement in order to reinforce the mobilization of this kind of clear class struggle? If I take the actions of the high school adolescents and the climate actions: this is absolutely stunning. But I see very few attempts from critical intellectuals at the elite's attempt at recuperating the movement. And the mainstream liberal argument is, 'You see politicians, what needs to be done? We need urgent techno-managerial change if we want to really deal with the climate!' Nonetheless, most of us *know* that we can't deal with the climate catastrophe through institutional and technical means, that we need a social transformation. We know that! So why don't we tell both those high school students and the analysts who try to win them for their cause, that what is needed is social transformation? Why don't we tell them that changes in the way we organize our energetic configuration, that neither technology nor the democratization of the market is going to bring this transformation? Where are these voices that speak to that kind of message, rather than trying to recuperate the life force of those kids that are fighting for something else (rather than for techno-managerial solutions that do nothing)?

Audience: Every one of us here in this room will end up taking some kind of position that might be influential. And it makes a difference whether we know the different fields wherein the battle is being fought (ideologically, economically, politically and so on). For example, some of us think that it's the very small things that we do that can and do make a difference.

Bob Jessop

Let's take the World Economic Forum. When they're doing their risk reports, they are identifying real-world problems from a multi-dimensional, multi-disciplinary perspective and asking, 'What are we going to do about it?' But of course, they want to solve those problems on behalf of transnational capital. They want to deal with the climate in terms of carbon trading, and things like that. But what the people in favour of social innovation, or radical social transformation, need to do is to work with the same risks—but from the viewpoint of the oppressed, deprived and exploited. As I said, we can identify where the weak points are, to come up with alternative, practical solutions, identify where at the local level or regional level solutions are being found, and then get maximum publicity to boost the ability to connect with each other, to link up with social movements and so forth. So not a meta-Davos but a meta-Oxfam, so to speak, because Oxfam is coming up with the more bottom-linked and bottom-up perspectives on all these problems and suggesting other solutions (what the Oxfam report does is to show how this problem is being solved here and there). It seems to me that one of the biggest failings of left intellectuals, of organic intellectuals, is the inability to engage with practical examples of solutions to real-world problems, and then meet with those and advance them.

Frank Moulaert

As a good Christian, I have a good conscience and will sleep very well tonight!

I didn't get an answer to my question: what will make the change in numbers? I think this needs a lot more reflection and a lot more interaction with the social and political movements. I think it's an unanswered question and we really have to keep working on this.

Bob Jessop

There is a non-real answer which you refer to, which is the need for dialectical thinking: the transformation of quantity and quality, which answers nothing unless you get a sufficiently rich and wide-ranging number of movements in dialogue (rather than the same movement talking to the same movement on a single issue).

Frank Moulaert

We should dare to believe that movements that are socially innovative can have a politically transformative impact. I keep giving the example of VELT (a bio-agricultural organization) in Flanders and the Netherlands, which unites to a certain extent, professional gardeners, agricultural professionals, leisure time gardeners, amateurs and so on, ...[4] VELT has had a growing impact on environmental consciousness. It influences the way we deal with food and food provision. Could such movements play an important role in the building of a social political movement, or are they *already* having an impact on the building of a social political movement that could inspire *another* type of democratic system that takes into account many more voices?

And turning now to 'us': who is us? We are speaking of a complex composition of society, we have referred to class composition, to social differentiation, and we can add cultural identities and so on. All of these are very differentiated and I think we all have different roles within societal dynamics. If you talk about organic intellectuals, it means something different for you than it does to me. I mean, I could see Erik Swyngedouw standing on a soapbox in Paris (your French would have to get a lot better to get things to happen faster). I can see Bob Jessop's role as being much more that of the meta thinker who can put our different ways of approaching things together, putting them in interaction. And I think I'm much more the educator who tries to transform (and I'm sorry I think in such instrumentalist manipulative terms) my PhD students into activists, or teach them how to organize a research team or research network in such a way that it is useful for social political transformation in different ways.

Bob Jessop

So, you've just given me an opportunity to turn a joke from my students into a useful illustration. They say, 'Anything you can do, Bob can do meta.'

Erik Swyngedouw

I very much believe that we all have our own specific function within the social world. Politically speaking, though, I would argue that there is an 'us' and a 'them'. By 'us', politically speaking, I mean those who believe or have faith that a free, equal and ecologically sane society is not only possible, but absolutely necessary. That's the 'us', irrespective of our different social positionality within the world. By 'them' I mean those who by all means possible will make it *impossible* for the world to become more free, equal and ecologically sane. So, I do think there is a separating line. Of course, what distinguishes 'us' from 'them' is that we extend an infinite invitation to everyone to join us. So, the question is, of course, what do we do with those who refuse the invitation and the line that we draw? How do we deal with these 'others' that insist on preserving the status quo? This is perhaps something that we share.

We were arguing earlier that the proletariat never was perhaps a majority and now in the global North is a minority; for so many dogmatic Marxists that seems to be an issue. However, if we consider the contemporary dynamic of capitalism, aren't we all being increasingly proletarianized (turned into proletarians)? But not in the way in which the industrial proletariat was exploited (they were exploited as Marx explained through the production process, and that still happens, that won't disappear: China is a good case and India is following rapidly). Here and in many other places, capital accumulation unfolds in what David Harvey would call 'accumulation by dispossession'. This is a completely different way through which people are proletarianized than through the capitalist labour process: their land is stolen—and this is as old as economic exploitation itself, their ecologies destroyed, their houses mortgaged and integrated in a global financial circuit. Elsewhere, our most intimate moments are being turned into a commodity. I mean, if you use Spotify (or other social media), you know Spotify is making money on your listening: it's packaging my choice and preferences. Be it Google or any of these other social platforms, it is dispossessing us, not just of our time (as it did with the standard proletariat), but also from our totality of being and turns our deepest feelings and sentiments into a commodity. These processes constitute a range of disempowering and proletarianizing dynamics that operate through generalized dispossession, and this might be a wedge through which new alliances and new forms of class struggle are waged.

Frank Moulaert

Another process of mobilization would be that linked to the health consequences of the climate issue. Middle-class people who vote conservatively may now start to vote green, because they understand that bad air quality affects the health conditions of their kids. And that's an argument that enters the mind of many people.

Bob Jessop

Listening to you, perhaps the umbrella concept here is sustainability (linking all of the different struggles around a very broad and wide range of issues related to sustainability).

Referring to your comments on increasing dispossession: this also explains why there's a retreat from democracy. Paraphrasing Marx: where exploitation takes the form of exchange, dictatorship may take the form of democracy; but where exploitation takes the form of politically mediated dispossession, democracy becomes really difficult because there's a fusion of the economic and the political elites. I was reading in *The Economist* just two days ago that 70 per cent of the world's GDP is found in countries where authoritarian leaders (including, for example, Trump) are in charge of their respective economy. The idea that capitalism goes hand in hand with democracy is now completely false (even if it were true in the late nineteenth, very early twentieth century). This is one of the illusions we need to get rid of, which is why I think your arguments around the post-political, at least in the sense of the post-democratic political, are more and more relevant.

5.6   On social innovation and individualism

Audience: What if the polarized conditions for ensuring the success of socially innovative ideas don't exist? Is it possible for change to happen on an individualized level? Where I come from, there is little polarization: everybody deals individually with their problems, and to work on bringing some common understanding or common movement is difficult. But the problems are still there. So do we always have to go with this type of polarization or can an individual sometimes influence a different type of initiative, one that can lead to change?

Bob Jessop (i.e. 'the man in the middle'!)

I think the discourses are polarized, but I don't think the practices are polarized because they're much more ambivalent, and much more uncertain. One of the things I talk about in my reflection piece is the dilemma and the contradiction of the pressure around self-emancipation versus self-responsibilization. There is always the possibility of a self-emancipatory movement being captured and turned into a form of self-responsibilization. But equally movements that start out as saying, 'The markets failed. The states failed. We're handing things to you', can through their own dynamic develop in a very different direction.

Take the example of Britain in the 1960s: because of market failures and State failure, the Labour government at the time set up community development projects where they empowered local people to discuss their needs, and so forth, and thought they would be very responsible and work within the logic of the market and work within the logic of the State. Instead, people came up with non-negotiable, radical demands. The government then closed the community development projects down. So, I think that even though the discourse may be polarizing, there's a lot more potential in self-emancipatory and self-responsibilizing initiatives to turn one way or the other. And that brings us back to the importance of the politics/politicization discussions, and of bringing about an opening up to possibilities of risks and opportunities of different kinds of bottom-linked movements.

Frank Moulaert

I think that it is important to share with you that we, as speakers, have known each other for a long time. And when we listen to each other, we always learn something new. What I hear from Erik Swyngedouw and Bob Jessop helps me to articulate my own thoughts and leads me to new questions. So that's part of the intellectual activity and responsibility that we undertake. But this also leads me to criticize this form of communication: we are very respectful people to each other and we didn't have time to really digest the new messages that we brought to each other this morning and afternoon. So, a debate of this kind would be even more interesting, a few days later (but then there is the problem of time and availability, etc.).

Notes

1. The debate was organized as part of the International Module in Spatial Development Planning in KU Leuven's Planning & Development.
2. See FEBA reports on this at https://www.eurofoodbank.org/.
3. N. Poulantzas (1978). *State, Power, Socialism*. New Left Books.
4. See https://velt.be/.

6   Towards Socially Innovative Political Transformation

Frank Moulaert, Pieter Van den Broeck, Liana Simmons, Bob Jessop and Erik Swyngedouw

The contemporary relationship between the social—in the sense of building society based on mutual aid and collective care—and the political, in the sense of returning to democratic political decision-making instead of public management by expert elites, is fragile. This Dialogue book has discussed this fragility. It examines strategies to turn this fragile relationship into proactive political actions and to build a nurturing socio-political dynamic that reinvigorates political life—one that is predicated on transforming the State from a control system promoting economic individualism and entrepreneurship of the self to a system based on universal emancipation and collective solidarity. In such a system, self-emancipation, with self-responsibilization as part of a collective bottom-linked emancipation process—the core of social innovation—would be part of a process of solidarity building instead of a disciplining tool of the control State.

This conclusion proceeds in four steps. In Section 6.1, we summarize what we learned in previous chapters about the state of 'the political' today. In Section 6.2, we focus on civil society, its political roles, and the various forms they take. We examine the change potential of civil society and how nurturing its diversity can produce socio-political change. This section explains how self-emancipation, as one of the main driving forces in social innovation and political mobilization movements, transforms the meaning of self-responsibilization within the neoliberal State system to self-responsibilization as a factor of self-emancipation in the sense of 'doing yourself what you have to do' in order to return the principles of solidarity to society. Section 6.3 examines the fragility of change strategies emerging from civil society seeking to find a workable balance between social innovation (return to mutual aid, building deep democracy organizations, bottom-linked governance and so on) and political mobilization. The concluding Section 6.4 highlights the conditions under which socially innovative initiatives and movements can have a greater socio-political transformative impact and under which political movements can valorize more their social potential. The focus here is on considering the mutually nurturing interaction between innovative social experiments, on the one hand, and universalizing procedures of political transformation, on the other. We conclude with 'Contrapunti', presenting remaining questions, remaining contradictions and hints on how to overcome them.

6.1   What remains of the political?

The malfunctioning of political life and the shortcomings of the contemporary State apparatus are well known and have been well documented in the reflection chapters in this book. As causes of these conditions, citizens commonly refer to the incompetence of politicians and political personnel, their pursuit of self-interest, their collusion with the business and financial world, their short-sightedness and, perhaps most of all, their lack of empathy with people engaged to overcome their current ecological, social and economic problems. It is a euphemism to say that the political has moved away from a large part of society and that the concerns felt in the (under)belly of society are no longer considered by the majority of politicians as politically important. What they consider relevant is the information that 'comes in' through the channels of the technocratic knowledge society. The Covid-19 debate and the fundamental disagreement about the social price of the climate crisis are probably the most prominent examples of the abyss between politicians and the people. A decent income and housing for all, clean water, pure air, healthy and clean public spaces, preventive health care, have tumbled down the rungs of the political priority ladder. 'Why can't the State spend as much money on dealing with these ecological and social problems as on fighting Covid-19?' is a question many citizens ask these days. But even if the State were willing to spend the necessary resources to tackle these essential problems, it would not solve the crisis of the State, because the State has, since the return of liberalism, increasingly excluded participatory political dynamics from its institutions and agency. The re-politicization of the State, in the sense of reinvigorating its democratic processes and returning to its societal mission (i.e. providing a voice and welfare for all) will have to come from outside the State, as, for example, expressed by Erik Swyngedouw who focuses on the performative effect of the 'political as it unfolds at a distance from the State' (Chapter 3, p. 61). He writes:

> The mutual re-enforcing of mobilizations at a distance from the State and transforming institutional arrangements within the State constitute the vector through which transformative practices become both enacted and institutionalized. However, the insurgent actions [...] are rarely performative in terms of altering the politico-institutional configuration, and in particular, in really nudging the deepening of austerity and neoliberalism towards a more inclusive, socially and ecologically sensible way of governing. In fact, I would argue that there is an increasing gulf opening up between insurgent movements, on the one hand, and the act of governing, on the other, something that might lead to further radicalization of insurgent activities. (Chapter 3, p. 63)

This comment highlights how the contemporary State differs from the pre-modern State explored in Chapter 1. Indeed, in Western society, from the late Middle Ages onwards, the political has evolved from local community-based shared decision-making and leadership (applying mutual aid to satisfy community needs on a more or less consensual basis) to a top-down nationwide political system pursuing the centralization of values and social relations as well as fake responsibilization—fake in the sense that responsibility is assessed in terms of respect of market criteria and State-established rules. Many of these State-established rules only exist for the sake of controlling citizens and migrants in many different ways, instead of taking collective responsibility for general well-being through community building, people's health, climate action, civil society mobilization and so on. In this way, responsibilization is ontologically reduced to obeying the rules of market and State, which in the end boils down to avoiding fines and shirking duties. This attitude easily generalizes into indifference towards collective State initiatives and participation in collective decision-making. For indeed, rebuilding collective responsibility through civil society initiatives and the like will only succeed by rejecting or transforming many of the existent State rules, such as free trade agreements, bureaucratic practices in treating the poor and unemployed, rules setting the use of public space, absurd bureaucratic practices in most domains of public administration and so on. But it will also require reversing the social psychology of following imposed rules and the attitude of self-preservation that comes from seeking to avoid individual sanctioning by the police State (see Chapter 3, p. 70). In short, interrupting or transgressing the institutionalized functioning of the State is seen as a prerequisite for the formation and nurturing of different political strategies and trajectories.

6.1.1 How to Create Space for Democratic Responsibilization?

The longue durée development of the political that occurred since the rise of regal autocracy has especially meant a reduction of the political to politics, and of socio-political governance to public management according to micro-economic criteria. The growing responsibilization of citizens by the steadily centralizing State system has made them accountable for obeying State-imposed rules, many of which stem from a logic of private economic interest, with the sacrosanct respect for any type of private property; this often perverts into widespread individualist, self-centred practices and competitive behaviour. Discouraging illustrations include segregation through education in elite schools, land consumption leading to low-density suburbanization, speculative housing investment by middle-class owners, occupation of nature reserves by second homes and so on.

The top-down disciplining relationship between State and citizens, a hierarchical relationship that developed together with the rise of the central State (Chapter 1), fosters an inherently non-economic aspect of individualism, that is, being responsible as an individual vis-à-vis the law and State institutions and being controlled by the State in terms of this 'responsibility'. This has also reinforced economic individualism, that is, the pursuit of one's own economic interest in different life spheres and their commodifying markets (labour, real estate, general consumption goods, health, education ...). The combination of both forms of individualization (pursuit of economic self-interest, protecting individual civil rights by respecting imposed State rules) has reinforced the systemic integration of market society and State control.

The State's appeal for greater responsibility of citizens clashes (in a contradictory manner) with the pretended modes of communication of the contemporary State, which, while trying hard to keep up the appearances of being open and democratic through its discourses on inclusion and respect for diversity, remains hegemonic in imposing system-preserving rules; a system dominated by technological and micro-economic logic, but weak in recognizing and valorizing popular dynamics. How can a system responsibilize people if it limits their freedom of expression and political behaviour? The way most Western democracies have managed the Covid-19 crisis speaks loudly of this contradiction: alternative voices on health care and policy are shut down, the urgent return to the 'old' economy post-Covid is heralded from dawn to dusk, the media have reached a type of self-censorship and focus their communication on official or system-obedient voices (with some tolerance for voices 'questioning the mainstream' and 'noise' in the background). In other words, the so-called 'responsible' citizens are not allowed to form their own opinion on how public action should proceed, the (yes, authoritarian) State tells them how to think and behave. A large part of the population will disagree with this observation because they have stopped critical thinking as they have become straightjacketed into this socio-technical logic or are existentially forced to focus on their place in the treadmill of socio-economic survival.

The deepening symbiosis between State and economy and the destructive impact this has on both society and polity have been analysed by many authors. In Polanyi's terms, the State is less and less embedded in society, and increasingly embedded in the (global) economy in which it has taken on more public management roles to ensure society smoothly fits into the competitive economy, with freedom of investment and trade being guaranteed. The State has largely become a conglomerate of agencies, a technocracy preserving and promoting private sector and public administration interests or working out compromises between economy and society to make sure the former can persist in growth strategies that destroy both planet and society. This focus on the smooth regulation of the market economy is materialized in new public management (NPM) tools used by State institutions to steer the economic feasibility of State initiatives; these institutions are being organized and function according to economic governance principles. As such, the State is dictated solely by its economic and control (rather than democratic) functions, which in turn leads to great discontent among citizens who desire a democratic control of all types of State functions (such as guaranteeing constitutional rights or keeping citizens' rights and governance principles at the heart of the public (political) debate). In the name of solving financial crises, health crises and dealing with terrorism, 'democratic procedures are suspended and assumedly unavoidable measures are implemented (Chapter 3, p. 64). Blank votes, absenteeism, radical voters calling for more rights for the local population and/or the socially, economically and politically excluded across Europe amount to between 30 per cent and 50 per cent of the 'voters'. These (non)voters all want a more democratic State, but the State walks on the leash of big capital and hard science, avoiding pluralist debate, as if what mainstream economists or scientists defend as solutions to collective problems represent one big truth. Such tactics disavow the possible emergence of different truth-regimes, predicated on a different set of assumptions, visions and aspirations.

The oligopolistic and monopolistic players in the private sector rule the waves of socio-economic change. Alternative initiatives and organizations are minimized within the context of a global, megalomaniac discourse and technocratic policy view of how the world should move in the future. A telling illustration of this megalomania is the pursuit of Green New Deal proposals. This wide variety of proposals is overwhelmingly technologically calibrated; the disastrous state of social and political relations is completely absent from the picture of the socio-ecological systems in which we 'live'.[1] Yet political ecologists and analysts of socio-ecological systems stress the key role of social relations, alternative political governance and social innovation in transformative strategies. Still the focus is squarely on socio-technical transition to keep the existing politico-economic order intact rather than on the political conditions of socio-ecological transformation. But should we be that harsh on the State and its institutions? As many analysts would argue, this capitalist State has produced the welfare State: 'More substantively, there is a role for the State in the care economy, in reproduction and in generating revenues that can be turned into benefits for civil society' (Chapter 4, p. 74). This is still true today. But even in these roles, the State currently applies criteria of financial accountability and bureaucratic responsibilization in terms explained above. And because of its growing collusion with the economic world, the State seems to have lost the power and instruments to let the economy serve the social—or seems to reduce the meaning of the social to providing material well-being for all. Material well-being is no longer understood in terms of equity or ecological quality, but in terms of 'well-being for whoever deserves it through his/her economic performance' and as benign charity for those who do not deserve it. But such an interpretation of the welfare State is even too gentle, as witnessed by the millions of working poor who work their health away while making an income that in Western 'welfare' countries does not reach the minimum welfare income (see, for example, Andress and Lohmann 2008).

But there is another side of the social—building community within a healthy socio-ecological environment—that is still State-supported financially through cultural and educational policy. But here again the managerial logic predominates. State funding and official recognition of socio-cultural and environmental organizations depend on their respect for NPM rules. Even education, from primary schools to postgraduate training, has to fit that logic and achieve educational 'end goals' instead of promoting collective learning in which communication, listening capacity, handling differences and conflict-resolution are high up on the agenda (through, for example, project education). Another missed opportunity, as collective learning from the primary school on would be a great opportunity to educate proactive citizens, caring about building community and reinforcing democracy.

The relationship between State and society can only be transformed in the direction of enhanced emancipation and collective responsibilization by reviving political dynamics in which all citizens have a stake in pursuing equality. What is or should be the role of social and political movements in reviving these dynamics? What about citizenship? Movements for political and social change are emerging in different parts of the world. Timid attempts to transform existing political parties or to create new ones have so far failed to change the trajectory of the future, coming up against the logic of parliamentary governance based on law-making within the boundaries of 'market democracy' (Chapter 4, p. 85). In contemporary terms, such governance means that laws and regulations should conform to the socio-technical logics of the prevalent market order. They should fit the socio-technical foundations on which Western societies are alleged to function today—a detrimental hollowing out of the diverse aspects of rationality as expressed in humanism and in the foundations of the Enlightenment—and give predominance to hard science in R&D policy and economic development models over universality in knowledge acquisition and building polity. Laws and regulations should be written and enacted within the contours of public management budgetary austerity and adaptive governance rules, vigorously blocking off the redistribution of income and wealth and pluralist views of human well-being. Within such a reductive 'decision space', no sustainable climate or social cohesion policy is possible. This impossibility is reflected, for example, in the structural gap between the official lip service given to repairing the disastrous state of the environment (the ridiculous 'real' commitments to preserving so-called eco-system services and the global market for emission rights as the only 'realistic' solution) and the absolute absence of the social and political dynamics of the (socio-)ecological system change in any of the Green New Deal proposals (Kenis and Lievens 2015).

In this far from rosy context, socially innovative initiatives in most life spheres have managed to address unsatisfied collective and individual needs, build mutual-aid social relations, and work with bottom-linked governance modes involving local authorities in co-learning and co-production processes. Many of these initiatives have laid the basis of socio-political movements standing up for housing rights, minimum income, welfare for all, environmental restoration, recalibration of democratic rights in the socio-political system, human and minority rights and so on. Over decades of hard mobilizing work, socio-political movements created by socially innovative organizations at the local level have managed to occupy the political stages and 'conquer' city halls (Barcelona, Zagreb, ...; Eizaguirre et al. 2017; *Le Monde diplomatique* 2021). Examples include mass mobilizations such as the Anti-Eviction movement in Spain, the Occupy! movement across the Western world, the Arab Spring, the gilets jaunes in France and Belgium, and the anti-Covid-19 passport demonstrations (most of which are not directed against the vaccination policy per se but against the controlling State extorting personal will and responsibility from citizens). Do these more or less promising initiatives of social innovation and socio-political transformation show the way forward for rebuilding socio-political dynamics? The authors of the reflection chapters have complementary opinions on this question. These opinions are strongly related to the different, yet often compatible, meanings and especially roles of diverse fractions in civil society.

6.2   The potential of civil society for socio-political transformation

Following historical Marxism (e.g. Lukács 1972; Mandel 1972; Demirovic 1992) or Polanyi's historical sociology (Polanyi 2001 [1944]), the history of the world can be analysed as a dialectics of movements and counter-movements. The authors of the reflection chapters share this basic insight as a significant part of the (r)evolution of society. They stress that the interaction between economy, society and nature, generally recognized as the key domains around which these movements mobilize, has changed significantly since Polanyi's time. Despite the fascist counter-movement of the 1920s and 1930s, which reinforced the control of the State and imposed racist nationalism, Polanyi was hopeful about the re-embedding of the economy in society. With the Keynesian National Welfare State, his anticipations were partly realized. But some 20 years after he passed away (†1964), the wolf of liberalism returned wearing the sheep clothes of neoliberalism, whose desocializing features are well known. More than ever, in the last quarter of the nineteenth century and the first of the twentieth, society has become subordinated to the economy. Rarely has Marx's dictum that the economy determines social configurations been so close to reality. Social relations have become increasingly commodified—but see White (2009). People's minds (in their different roles in economy, society and polity) have become impregnated by values connected to the pursuit of self-interest such as income, wealth, security, NIMBY nesting, personal and household health, … By this, we do not mean that sociality has been reduced to social relations serving self-interest only, but that the mutual aid-based community building aspirations have become dominated by the State solidarity system, especially the welfare State. This process has reduced the importance of person-to-person and group-to-group solidarity relations, downgraded the political role of civil society organizations outside the State and augmented the power of pressure groups representing oligopolistic capital. As we explained in Chapter 1 and earlier in this chapter, the welfare State evolved into a welfare bureaucracy with needs—not often clear whose needs (those of the administrators or those of the needy)—being basically satisfied according to merits or tangible health conditions; in other words, it evolved into a bureaucracy functioning according to NPM principles, derived mostly from business administration manuals. Solidarity dynamics have occupied a marginal position, albeit less so in political discourse than in actual political practice (although the almost ubiquitous dismissive positioning of State discourse against refugees is an exception).

As discussed above, the roles of people as citizens, as political beings, have become highly de-politicized. The image of the 'market for votes' powerfully visualizes what this means. If humans as political beings are reduced in their behaviour to voting for themes on a political programme, this also means that they liberate themselves of the collective 'duty' or 'commitment' to take responsibility to become involved in some part of the socio-political governance of the polis. This may be good news for a public management-based government regime: as voting has become a kind of 'clicktivism' (Chapter 4, p. 79), people become less involved in what governments and public administrations do. The movement of people away from what States do takes many forms: the apathy many people report, expressed as 'politics don't interest me'; a lack of political interest, such as abstaining from voting because 'politicians do not serve the general interest anyway'; voting for populist and neo-fascist parties; or mobilizing for a change of and in socio-political structures and institutions. Such mobilizing can take many shapes, with different roles for civil society from which they are nascent. This is not to say that civil society is immune to bureaucratization and State control. Many organizations in the socio-cultural sector have turned into subsidy hunters, chasing subsidies that they can only acquire by respecting NPM and political correctness norms. Such conditions undermine the creativity of these organizations and their potential to have a political change role. This makes us nostalgic of independent *Volkshochschulen* like Elker-Ick in Flanders, which decades ago had a significant impact on the political debates on education, emancipation, gender and ethnic equality and so on.

Social life, especially through its different civil society movements and organizations, is experimenting with new forms of being political, that is, collectively governing communities and their networks, and looking for reliable and sustainable forms of democratic leadership. But in the course of history, civil society has received many meanings. Neera Chandhoke provides a hasty synthesis: Tocqueville refers to civil society as the realm of social associations; Gramsci considers it as the space where capitalist hegemony is (re)produced. And other authors have their understanding of civil society as well:

> A Hegelian worries that civil society is neither wholly good nor entirely bad, for it is the site of the battle between particularity and universality. An orthodox Marxist who has not taken Gramsci seriously would dismiss civil society as the sphere of the sale and the buying of labour power. And an economist hijacking Adam Smith's complex formulations in the *Wealth of Nations* [without reading his *The Theory of Moral Sentiments*] would employ the concept of civil society as synonymous with the capitalist economy. (Chandhoke 2009, p. 86)

In contemporary usage, she writes, 'civil society has become a tiresomely "hurrah" word hijacked by donor agencies, rendered synonymous with the non-governmental sector, and seen as a substitute for a non-performing State and a profit driven market.' Focusing on its relation to the State and the State-Market nexus, Bob Jessop in his Chapter 4 stresses the political roles of civil society (see also Jessop 2020). He asks two interrelated questions, one referring to a radical positioning towards the control of the State and market society, the other to what we used to call a 'reformist' view of the role of civil society leading towards a caring liberalism.

Bob Jessop writes:

> More recent discourses around civil society highlight the pluralist self-organization of civil society. Can this compensate for market and State failure in order to sustain the neoliberal project in the current conjuncture? Can it resist the colonization by the State or the encroachment of market forces and promote self-emancipation? At stake here is the tension between self-responsibilization and a pluralist, more solidaristic, self-emancipation project. (Chapter 4, p. 75)

The first question refers to the possibility of a counter-movement to neoliberalism in the Polanyian sense. The second question refers to how civil society could play a compensatory role in the neoliberalization of society given the relationship between the economic, social and political in the neoliberal society. Indeed, 'the tension between pluralist self-organization/self-responsibilization and the pluralist, more solidaristic, self-emancipation project' (Chapter 4, p. 86) is the most politically relevant question to be asked today.

Some sources stress the increasing separation between the economic, social and political spheres of society. This almost sounds contradictory to Polanyi's vision of (dis)embedding. But Polanyi referred to two historical periods of disembedding and re-embedding. The first was the freeing of economic relations from traditional social obligations, enabling the free market to operate in relation to land, labour power and money. The second was society's fightback and the re-embedding of the market economy in a market society that subjects market forces to social control. Nowadays, neoliberalism narrows the behavioural and institutional logics of the economic, political and social spheres due to the dominance of commodification and hierarchical control. For example, Bob Jessop flags up the 'economization of the economic struggle' (Chapter 4, p. 76) and the 'parliamentarization of political struggle' (Chapter 4, p. 80). The first means that only (market) economic instruments and discourses are used to fight for income and wealth and that when economic struggle threatens profits and employment, the struggle for wages is relaxed. Other than material benefits, values such as social struggles over equal rights and democratic economic organization are left out of the picture; and political struggles that focus on a just and socio-ecologically sustainable economic system are also ignored. The 'parliamentarization of political struggle' means a reduction of political life to salon elite debates and public management and the struggle for parliamentary majorities within the rules of universal suffrage. Most MPs generally uncritically internalize public management philosophy and hard science-based innovation. Accordingly, the State apparatus has become compartmentalized into agencies whose mission is defined in terms of quantifiable impact and evaluated by use of accountability procedures. The influence of mass mobilization that contests parliamentary democratic rules and seeks to employ economic coercion (e.g. general strikes) to influence government has become marginal; 'just wait till the storm is over' has become the common reaction pattern of the ruling elites.

Socio-political transformation will require surmounting this compartmentalization of the arenas of socio-political debate and struggle. This means not only surmounting the partitioning of the economic, political, social, ecological and cultural life-worlds, but also identifying the essence of their typical agencies and value systems throughout history (e.g. from mutual aid-based communities in the early Middle Ages to welfare statism and socio-cultural organization in post-industrial metropolises). Especially worrisome is the changed meaning of economic behaviour—from local divisions of labour and face-to-face exchange systems based on reciprocity and association, to global markets based on formal competition at all levels and in all life spheres. The destructive impact of economic life on other life spheres justifies this special focus. The dynamism of the diverse initiatives in the Third and Fourth sector of the 'alternative' economy witnesses almost organic reactions against the devastating impact of contemporary business practices on the psyche, creativity and sense of doing well of workers and managers (Moulaert and Ailenei 2005; Jessop and Sum 2019).

Civil society, in its definitional diversity, is present and active in these different life spheres. It employs different strategies and follows different logics to conserve and change social relations (again, in their diverse meanings) within and across these spheres. In this Dialogue, we wanted to identify and critically assess the role of civil society in embedding mutual aid and civilian responsibilization in socio-political dynamics. To turn State-regulated responsibilization into bottom-linked self-responsibilization requires a highly self-emancipatory civil society with organizations that are strongly engaged in democratic (self-)governance, political education and communication, building change agendas seeking to reconnect the various life spheres and networking with similar or complementary organizations to build socio-political movements.

These civil society organizations, by virtue of their private juridical character and their separation from the juridico-political State, can also be a source of resistance to economic exploitation and political domination. The organizations' self-emancipation is probably the key mechanism in building counter-hegemonic projects, breaking through the straightjacket of the control State and global market competition—both of which, we recall, foster individualist responsibilization and disembody societal solidarity from its essential mechanisms of solidarity, compassion and mutual aid. The re-scripting of emancipation over the past few decades in the direction of the promise of realizing individual enjoyment shifted the terrain of emancipation from a collective movement for equality to one centred around capsular isolation and ring-fencing of the individual body from allegedly harmful external intruders (Swyngedouw 2021).

Self-emancipation, in contrast, should, as far as possible, limit free market competition, serve as a control against over-influential monopolies and favour social enterprise and social surplus generation (not just profit generation). Rather than deregulation, it should promote empowerment—enhancing the role of the people by linking direct and representative democracy. Rather than privatization, it should advance socialization based on solidarity and reciprocity—expanding the social economy with an emphasis on social use-value in economic activities rather than on exchange-value, profitability and so on. It should not pursue free trade as much as promote fair trade. In other words, self-emancipation transforms self-responsibilization into a powerful strategy of resistance. It contests the neoliberal logic of the one-sided emphasis on exchange-value and the disciplinary logic of authoritarian Statism by emphasizing social use-values and the need to combine direct and representative democratic mobilization.

6.3   Unlocking the potentialities of civil society

But is this trust in the self-emancipatory power of certain civil society movements and networks exaggerated? The interlocutors in this Dialogue book do not offer a unified answer to this question, and hence there is no recipe book for change being offered as such. Nonetheless, what comes to the fore here—propelling us to consider the question of 'where to from here'—are the common components (or 'ingredients', to bring the recipe metaphor a step further) that stir, provoke and ferment this change.

As mentioned in our introduction, the plethora of socially innovative initiatives that can be found today (fostering citizen participation, grassroots democracy or direct democracy) are simply not bringing about democratizing political change. In other words, socially innovative initiatives are not converging with the rise of new grassroots 'political' experimentations; in the rare occasions that they do intersect, they remain painfully localized or their networks too sector-limited (food provision, shelter, …). This Dialogue book has unravelled the reasons behind this apparent contradiction, digging deep into the history and development of social and political life. In tackling the question of whether these movements can bring about socio-political transformation in a socio-ecologically inclusive and emancipatory way, differing angles are presented, which have to do with the nuts and bolts of democratizing political change. Bottom-linked governance is an attempt to make the convergence between social innovation and democratizing political change happen, and though the authors have a different take on the extent to which it is working and the extent to which we should set our hopes and dreams here, they agree on their fundamental and pivotal importance. In other words, though there may be threats (both internal and external) and innumerable risks of failure, it is in the self-emancipatory power of certain (universalizing) civil society movements and networks that we anticipate potential for change.

6.3.1   The Social Is Insufficiently Political

Social practices in themselves do not change the world; political practices may change the world, as Erik Swyngedouw claims. He argues that socially innovative experimentation, although a key and vital ingredient to nurture emancipatory social change, is politically non-performative without universalizing aspirations. More attention needs to be paid to the intellectual, not the least the theoretical and practical elements of political processes, and how these interact with and re-enforce new social forms: 'Political events rarely translate into a politicizing procedure that ends in institutional change and transformation.' He continues:

> We do know how this works historically. If you go back to the nineteenth century or twentieth century, it is clear how a political event occasionally turned into a collective emancipatory sequence: it was articulated through a privileged subject (the proletariat, who would *do* it), it had a particular form of organization (the political party; be it socialist or communist), which would be fighting to occupy the State. It produced the welfare State—an extremely significant, although imperfect, emancipatory social transformation. Most people today in the twenty-first century would argue that these three mechanisms do not work anymore. The proletariat as the preferential political subject is questionable; the hierarchical political party as the delivery organization is as dead as a donkey; and occupying the State is not going to do much either. The social innovation movement will not solve these dilemmas. (Chapter 5, pp. 97–98)

6.3.2   Under What Conditions Is Social Innovation Political?

Bob Jessop argues that Social Innovation (SI) should be insurgent and counter-hegemonic to become political, and break through the commodi-fication logic, public management approaches and so on. In a similar vein, drawing on extensive concrete examples as well as academic literature on SI and bottom-linked governance, Frank Moulaert insists that political potential resides in social practices and their capacity to transform the instituted order, especially through bottom-linked governance.

We can take this argument a step further by considering what bottom-linked governance entails. Social innovation incrementally pro-duces the political; the political is constituted by social innovation. There is no politicizing process without SI; the social is/can be political. Doing things socially different (more inclusively, in an ecologically sound manner, etc.) can be political, under certain conditions, building links with authorities, using the cracks, being disruptive, being strategic, acting through interruption, thinking about organization, being communica-tively smart and so on.

What exactly does this imply for activists, ideas, movements and institu-tions? Where is the arena where this politicizing process can take place? Frank Moulaert (Chapter 2, pp. 54–56) contends that social political transformation happens precisely in the processes of exchange, cooperation and co-learning between various organizations at interactive spatial scales; in particular, bottom-linked governance practices (drawn from experiments of mutual-aid ethics, democratic learning, networking, etc.) hold the potential of *transforming* the working of local governance. These in turn, can impact the working modes of the State apparatus at other spatial scales. The learning dynamics of bottom-linked governance involve the development of new forms of cooperation between actors and institutions across territorial scales in which policy (broadly defined) and other development practice are not dictated from any one level of governance but produced and institutionalized through interaction and cooperation itself. Bottom-linked governance starts from the concern that many new socially innovative initiatives are highly necessary but that their governance, as well as that of the relevant supportive as well as re-democratizing State institutions (in transition?), should be developed interactively. From this perspective, the recognition of civil society in multi-scalar governance is important, yet should be considered with care so as to prevent civil society's organizations becoming co-opted or forcing them to 'reduce their imaginative potential, to bridle their creativity or their subversive capacity' (De Schutter 2002, p. 216).

This does not come without its struggles: experiments in social and political practice are conflictual, often ineffective and involve deep co-learning—but these are key for reviving modes of solidarity, public participation and decision-making (De Schutter and Dedeurwaerdere 2021). As such, Frank Moulaert provocatively suggests that bottom-linked governance is in a way essential for a new political movement and for re-politicizing society. In fact, in different terms from those used by Erik Swyngedouw, Frank Moulaert retraces the building of the democratic welfare State, starting from the dynamism emerging from the social organizations and cooperative economy, which he considers the main triggers of the political socialist organizations and parties. Recall also that today SI experiences, organizations and networks, as well as reflective authors, are returning 'old' ethical discussions to the public arena; SI through its experimentation with rebuilding social bonds, satisfying unsatisfied needs and micro-political decision-making is also a prophylactic against doom mongering. Direct focus on the political without SI only nurtures depression and discouragement.

Bottom-linked socially innovative experiences are part of a wider movement that could lead to social political transformation based on a war of position (see Chapter 4). These SI initiatives include experimentation, new learning dynamics (on how democracy should work in society and in the polity that we dream of), a bold proliferation of movements and mobilization. Most bottom-linked governance practices occur in respectful cooperation between civil society organizations and local authorities. Many of them may be small but meaningful 'cases' of re-democratizing the (local) State (Moulaert et al. 2019; García and Moulaert 2022). The idea that building democracy is one thing and doing socially innovative initiatives is another thing is a dualistic and dangerous way of thinking.

Politicization processes involve social movements; this was also the case in the great social and political movements countering the ordeals of the Industrial Revolution. Without cooperatives, sewing circles, solidarity with widows and survivors of work accidents, pension savings cooperatives, the conscientization essential to successful political mobilizing would never have worked. Sure, many initiatives look Lilliputian. But there are numerous examples and for many of them the adagio 'I do not count! I am going to make it count!' is valid. There remains, however, the doubt on how to make it count politically.

6.3.3   How to Make Socially Innovative Initiatives Count—Politically?

Evidence from initiatives in SI and social enterprise bears an indication of the potential of civil society to develop sub-hegemonic projects, variations on the dominant theme, or counter-hegemonic projects. These projects actually contest, within the limits of the possible, the rule of capital and/or the power of the State. These forms of resistance are particularly important for subaltern groups and for old and new social movements that draw on networks and solidarity to resist market forces and the power of government.

As such, the struggle for hegemony is crucial and is also fought by and through socially innovative movements. Referring here to Gramsci is helpful to recall the unavoidable interdependence of social and political movements—which often cannot be reduced to a 'single' label—and the significance of historical dynamics. According to Gramsci, a war of position is the phase of slow, hidden conflict, where forces seek to gain decisive influence and power in society by building political, intellectual and moral leadership. Putting this insight in the context of Gramsci's epoch and his concern with democratic socialism, it involves a struggle to win bases of self-organized class power, to create a socialist vision in the working class and, in doing so, to build a counter-hegemonic discourse for the socialist movement. In contrast, '[a] war of manoeuvre is the phase of direct and open clashes between classes—not just eventual violent confrontation between the State and revolutionary forces. A war of position is the decisive struggle, even though it occurs before the open struggle that would be settled by force in a final military confrontation' (Chapter 4, p. 78).

Translating Gramsci's insights into the current conjuncture, we could argue that the war of position is still central to building SI as a means of self-emancipation. But it needs to take account of the rise of new media of communication, including social media, and the rise of the surveillance society and its algorithmic calculations and interventions. These transform the conditions for a war of manoeuvre. This requires the mobilization of a wide diversity of social organizations that are unified around different kinds of social innovation and different forms of struggle. Their unity is not based on a single shared identity but on the recognition of commonalities as well as differences in their respective forms of oppression and exploitation that enable support for and participation in common struggles with interdependent conditions and outcomes. This unity cannot be assumed as given in the manner that Erik Swyngedouw criticizes the old class-based politics of mobilization, but must be constructed through dialogue, mutuality and solidarity—oriented to creating conditions for self-emancipation. This requires most social forces to be organized in a bottom-led way under the leadership of a socially innovative cadre that aims to mobilize a wide variety of pluralist social forces. It may be necessary to fight an eventual war of politico-military manoeuvre against the forces of class coercion but this will be shorter and less violent if the conditions for social solidarity are created.

6.4   Ethics, moments of opportunity and socio-political transformation

The previous sections summarized the problematization of the relationship between SI (initiatives, movements) and socio-political transformation (politicizing initiatives, uprisings, interruptive movements).

This concluding section highlights the conditions under which socially innovative initiatives and movements can have a greater socio-political transformative impact and those under which political movements can valorize more their social potential. We cover five conditions. First, as this debate was mainly among reflexive activists (or activist intellectuals), we elaborate slightly on their engagement and what is expected from it. Second, we review what is 'new' in contemporary social movements and what this could mean for 'new' political ethics and citizenship. This again involves an important intellectual commitment. Third, we develop the issue of dispersal of social and political initiatives, their oft-mentioned Lilliputian impact and the ways to synergize these initiatives through reaching out, networking and cooperation. Fourth, we focus on moments of political opportunity (for example for transforming the State). Fifth, and finally, we nudge the debate on hegemonic and counter-hegemonic ideology further, to dwell on opportunities to return mutual aid to the prominent ethical status it needs 'to solve the problems of the world'.

6.4.1   Organic Intellectuals, Reflexive Activists

In his contribution (Chapter 3), Erik Swyngedouw emphasizes that critical intellectuals in the socio-political struggle overwhelmingly focus on the critical analysis of the situation, but customarily marginalize the strategic progressive political implications of their critique. In other words, there is an emphasis on social critique and a general silencing of critical political theory and praxis. Although many engaged intellectuals really embody Gramsci's paradox of the 'Pessimism of the intellect, optimism of the will', its translation into political strategy, tactics and modalities remains obscure.

Nonetheless, in addition to their critical and quite pessimistic conclusions about the future of humanity, many intellectuals have taken on significant roles in socially innovative initiatives and socio-political movements, as theorists and process analysts, as strategy advisors, mobilizing their experience in consultation and participation processes, as occupiers and movement (co-)leaders (Moulaert and Nussbaumer 2008). Many have joined movements that they knew might fail. Or as Bob Jessop writes in Chapter 4: 'The irony is that by choosing to fail, by mobilizing networks, solidarity, reflexive solidarity and so forth, you are reducing the risk of failure. This is a different way to interpret pessimism of the intellect, optimism of the will' (Chapter 4, p. 93). We suggest that, in order for socially innovative initiatives and movements to have a greater socio-political transformative impact, intellectuals must activate their analyses into veritable contributions, involving themselves in a holistic way in the complex nitty-gritty of these movements.

6.4.2 Socio-political Initiatives and New Political Ethics

The rather collective pessimism about the impact of the Lilliputian initiatives on socio-political change has obscured their innovative potential. This book was not meant as an encyclopaedia of such initiatives but the bibliography covering them (see e.g. Moulaert and MacCallum 2019; Jessop 2020; De Schutter and Dedeurwaerdere 2021; Vicari Haddock and Moulaert 2009) documents the proliferation and diversity of such initiatives. The wealth of (and diversity in) new practices in democratic governance (bottom-linked governance and others) is impressive. Bob Jessop warns against what he calls 'unicorn thinking' (Chapter 5, p. 106), reminding us that there is not one perfect design of governance but that variety is needed for flexibility, and that forms of governance need to be constantly questioned, monitored, and recalibrated: 'What's important is to create the space for people to learn from their (collective) experiences, correct their mistakes, to comment on different activities and move forward' (Chapter 5, p. 106).

Central messages from these experiences to the socio-political movements in general are: (i) there are a host of new governance practices that re-establish values of equality and solidarity into local governance and that can inspire innovative governance at other spatial scales; (ii) deep democracy involves respect for diversity; and (iii) the real impact of these innovations will only occur if citizenship is redefined in those terms. The latter will only happen through the emancipation processes in the diversity of movements, but also in the daily interaction between people—to move, for example, away from bourgeois courtesy to communal solidarity in neighbourhood relations. As Erik Swyngedouw attests:

> The emancipatory process is that which produces equality and freedom. By freedom, I am not speaking of freedom as 'the freedom of choice' (that is a liberal notion), but as the capacity to do what you *have* to do (not what you *choose* to do) because you have no other choice ... These notions of equality and freedom have to be historically continuously re-constituted, they have to be invented and reinvented. (Chapter 5, p. 104)

So, the very notion of emancipation is never fixed: it is continuously reinvented and redefined, and new forms of equality/inequality force themselves continuously onto the political agenda (Chapter 5, p. 104). In other words, we suggest that a pivotal element for socio-political transformation is the disposition of actors to engage deeply in this ever-changing notion of emancipation, undertaking genuine openness to redefining and repositioning their work accordingly (i.e. remaining constantly abreast and in tune with the current forms of equality/inequality).

6.4.3   Networking and Cooperation in Different Forms

In his contribution, Bob Jessop emphasizes that the mobilization of socially innovative practices to nurture socio-political transformation must rely primarily on networked relations and practices of solidarity rather than on markets or on hierarchy and command-based governance configurations as seen in the neoliberal State (which are based on sanctioned respect for laws and regulations fitting the logic of NPM). He stresses the importance of reaching out in shared conditions:

> And that's where social movements become important because they start to speak on behalf of not just a particular interest but *sets* of marginalized interests. And that's their strength and their potential: they don't just contest saying, 'We're being left out'; they say, 'We share a lot in common with other people who are being left out.' And that's the basis then for the mobilization of social initiatives of many kinds. (Chapter 5, p. 107–108)

It is from such universalizing moments that embryonic forms of politicization might emerge. Visualizing and sharing these 'commonalities' are important tasks for organizations and networks to show that 'Another world is possible.'[2]

6.4.4   Moments of Opportunity—Transforming the State: an Illusion?

In the political economic analysis implicit to the analysis in this book (Regulation Theory, DEMOLOGOS, time-space analysis; Jessop 1995; Martinelli et al. 2013; Moulaert et al. 2016; Jessop 2006), the importance of emblematic moments and turning points in historical trajectories is stressed. Retrospectively, the coincidence of conditions and factors that made the 'turn' happen are analysed. What or who made the Paris Commune happen? What led to the vote of the foundational laws of the welfare State in several Western countries? What created the conditions for bottom-linked neighbourhood development in Antwerp, Barcelona, Zagreb, Toronto, …? And which conditions were not met to sustain the first fragile steps of the socio-political change movements? Which steps need to be taken to deregulate the neoliberal State and market? Other interrelated questions have to do with how to multiply and synergize the impact of Lilliputian socially and politically innovative initiatives into real change movements; how to let deep democracy practices percolate into State (agency) practices; how to turn citizenship education into emancipatory empowerment. Although we have not addressed all of these in detail, we have given some answers to these questions in this Dialogue. The most challenging issues seem to be re-democratizing the State and the re-conscientization of people away from market fundamentalism in the direction of a mutual-aid ideology. We return to the latter in the next subsection. As to the State, Bob Jessop stresses the importance of redesigning the State by affording opportunities for local authorities to support socially innovative initiatives and of ensuring horizontal linkages to guarantee a transfer of best practice beyond the local. Redesigning the State apparatus is fundamental to enabling SI to occur and thrive. That should be, Bob Jessop argues, an important part of any social innovation, social economy and bottom-linked strategy. In other words, you need to redesign the State to enable it to support these initiatives and open up opportunities for improving democracy. There may or may not be struggles within the State over whether we should support it or not, but then the mobilization outside the State (which Erik Swyngedouw talks a great deal about) is also crucial. The distinction between the different relations between civil society and the State matters here. How can similar or connected organizations act against the State and the global market, and still be engaged in building bottom-linked governance, which is based on new forms of cooperation and organization between (local) government, State agencies and socially innovative organizations (see e.g. Paidakaki et al. 2020; Manganelli and Moulaert 2018; Eizaguirre et al. 2017)? In a complex society, diverse trajectories of emancipation unroll, often led or animated by the same organizations or movements; some of these involve civil society initiatives within the State, others without or even against it. Still, these trajectories 'meet' and their interactions work transformatively for the local State, local business and the SI organizations. An interesting trajectory that political economists often overlook is to confront (the) State (levels) when they do not respect their own laws and regulations, or abstain from approving international agreements meant to promote social cohesion. A recent case concerns Flemish (social) housing policy.

A consortium of 38 organizations is committed to start a legal procedure against Flemish housing policy, which despite the fact that the Flemish 'Housing Codex' (Vlaamse Codex Wonen) in spirit subscribes to Article 31 of the European Social Charter (specifically dealing with housing), in practice the Flemish housing policy fails to satisfy the massive need for social housing.[3] In sum, we suggest that it is here, in this node of unusual combinations, exceptions and collaborations of emancipatory trajectories (where solidarity finds unmistakable concrete forms) that potential for scaling up and out lies.

6.4.5 Hegemony and Counter-hegemony: the Role of Ideology and Discourse

When civil society pursues social and political transformation, it experiences the hegemony of market liberalism and NPM, which are both connected through neoliberalism (competition as the dominant human agency, solidarity reduced to State meritocracy) as the social force paralysing radical social and political change potential. This paralysing impact is dishearteningly tangible within the ideological battle fought in scientific and public media. Hegemonic world views and discourses rule the knowledge society, including the world of scientific research; we often feel powerless to feed messages of mutual aid and socio-ecological strategies into the ether and human minds. Over the last few decades, more than before, mainstream media have abandoned covering grassroots protests and initiatives or the destructive role of efficient management and hard science in dealing with societal problems; attention has primarily focused on sensational news (natural disasters, wars, the life of media stars, ...) and popularized official State, economy and technological 'good news'.

Alternative media has taken over covering people's fates, frustrations, acts of courage and tenacity but seldom does it reach the global communication channels. But the world of alternative media is as diverse as that of grassroots initiatives and other popular initiatives; fake and truthful truths abound, fake truths or self-censorship increasingly percolate official media while they refute politically truthful information as having the status of fake truth (e.g. on the role of banks in causing the housing crisis, the impact of the real estate sector and the energy sector on a failing climate policy, the relationship between 'chemical' agrobusiness and the decline of the general immunity of the population, the denigration of alternative medicine while it has saved hundreds of thousands of people in the Western world, ...). Alternative global and local websites fill some of the cracks, but new initiatives need to be taken to return the right for accurate information to the people. The role of organic intellectuals needs to be revisited in this matter. Scientific epistemologies, analytical frameworks and categories remain essential tools in scientific research. Instead of engaging in the publish or perish battle and seeking highest citation impact, organic intellectual should engage more in publicizing their views of the world, their scientific approaches and results. And if the mainstream media often remain closed to their messages, there always remains publishing books for the educated general public, the use of podcasts, open access websites and so on.

Against the backdrop of hegemonic market liberalism and NPM, and in the context of heightening despair over climate change and the lack of solidarity and open debate demonstrated in dealing with Covid-19, the longing for a counter-hegemonic discourse risks remaining just that—a longing. To return to the question posed at the beginning of this section: do these more or less promising initiatives of social innovation and socio-political transformation show the way forward for rebuilding socio-political dynamics? All the authors agree that yes, in part they do: they represent the raw material needed to redesign the system. Examples of bottom-linked forms of governance provide the signs of positive changes, and highlight the essential role that progressive institutions, among which sensitized civil servants as well as influential decision makers play in bringing about socio-political transformation. Whether these initiatives can outmanoeuvre the hegemonic discourse that entraps all matters social and political—all this is another question, which the more hopeful amongst us dare to push and the less hopeful caution against (lest we fall into utopian dreams). Whilst admitting to the inevitability of failure, as Bob Jessop warns, this Dialogue represents a proactive call for action (both inwards and outwards): in other words, this is not just a plea from ideologues of a past generation on a soul-searching mission. It is a battle cry that shouts 'in order for us to hold up the notion that another world is possible we must work better, more closely, more strategically, across institutions and disciplines, and keep our eyes open to what is happening in key meeting points of emancipatory trajectories.' We must find that fine balance between transformative and utopic objectives and pragmatic approaches, in order to challenge, subvert, transform.

6.5   Contrapunti

We are aware that although our debate converged on many points, it did not answer several remaining questions or analyse persistent contradictions. We now address three issues.

First, many if not most SI initiatives rely on resources provided by the State and allocated to them according to the handbook of NPM. Such a contradictory situation is possible because in most countries the State is not a monolithic bloc but a conglomerate of many arenas of socio-political struggles, with the actors of one agency at one scale of governance often counteracting those belonging to another agency at another level. There are various ways to look at this practice. SI literature in its case studies shows clearly that through bottom-linked governance, allocation of public funds has found collectively more useful destinations. These cases illustrate how civil society can be effective in changing State practices from 'within', yet steered from 'without'. State subsidies to or through civil society organizations do not automatically mean locking them into ideological obedience.

Second, if indeed we accept that bottom-linked governance is effective in changing governance practices and allocation of (local) public funds, we remain confronted with the neoliberal view of public spending stimulating the private sector through deregulation and tax advantages and its austerity policy. This view particularly concerns public spending for social and cultural purposes. Where socially and politically innovative local regimes were put in place in Spain, for example, they bumped into the straitjacket of the neoliberal national and regional State, refusing to increase the State budget for social housing, to name just one of the most urgent issues. Local bottom-linked initiatives and citizen budgeting will indeed not suffice to overturn neoliberal budgetary policy, or their technological and managerial approaches to managing State funding, to replace it by budget policy responding to collective needs. It will need a worldwide political movement to change the meaning of 'the economic' in State institutions and agency. One of this movement's major missions will be to politically redefine the role of public budgets, their financial sources and the procedures of collective management (see Kelton 2021, for example, and Engelen et al. 2017 on the foundational economy). In the building of such a movement, organizations and networks at all scales will matter. But as Erik Swyngedouw warns:

> The financial and political elites will mobilize whatever tactics they can to ensure that a movement does not shift from a localized uprising to a universalizing procedure. When a social movement has a chance of success, the elites' hammer comes down hard—it comes down with extreme violence. If we don't have an answer on how to deal with mobilized violence at moments that politicization succeeds, then we will find it very difficult to deploy effective political strategies for lasting political change. (Chapter 5, p. 99)

Third (and this brings us back to self-emancipation) in this Dialogue book, different types of self-emancipation initiatives were identified: political movements with different agendas, social enterprises, socially innovative initiatives in diverse spheres of society, bottom-linked governance and so forth. Under each of these labels, numerous specific subtypes can be identified. In most cases, these agencies refer to people collectively taking their fate and future in their own hands, not willing to depend on failing State and market allocation systems. People refute these allocation systems for different reasons: lack of resources to act in the regular markets, misallocation of public funds, suffocating control and sanctioning systems in both the market and the State. And probably most of all: adversity to the subjectivation process imposed by market and State ethics, rejecting a value system based on competitiveness and rule obedience.

For us, self-emancipation is the shared social feature of most bottom-up, bottom-linked or grassroots initiatives and movements that we have looked at. They are the most promising form of political engagement today. They practise in their operation and mobilization the forms of equality the authors in this book share. They have set up and practised new forms of organization, discussing and putting into action shared values, modes of communication and decision-making, thus positively valorizing the diverse value-added that the post-industrial society has produced. Through their grassroots democracy practices and forms of mutually transformative cooperation with local State agencies, they have thoroughly re-institutionalized local political life. But the proliferation of this self-emancipation, as the essential pillar for socio-political transformations, remains most often limited to the local level. Therefore, hard work lies ahead consisting of networking across different types of organizations, domains and forms of action. For intellectuals, this not only means dropping the jet-set style, but also abandoning publish and perish individualism; on a proactive note, this means they should further develop transdisciplinary action research (e.g. through operationalizing dialogical epistemologies), democratize university life (e.g. apply SI ethics to the working of research units and laboratories), popularize research methods and results (e.g. through general public books, podcasts, …). A much harder part of the reinvention of the 'organic intellectual' will be reconquering a place on the political stage. Politicians and public managers today have become so intellectually dull that they prefer to listen to the advice of consultants arriving overnight with a bucket list of 'things to do' rather than take time to discuss with scientists the complexity of a societal problem that needs to be addressed.

Notes

1. See Climate Action Network (https://climatenetwork.org/).
2. Most projects and networks of SI provide atlases, monographs and data-banks of social innovation. See, for example, the *Atlases of Social Innovation* (Volumes 1 and 2) edited by Jürgen Howaldt, Christoph Kaletka, Antonius Schröder and Marthe Zirngiebl; the Romanian atlas of social economy (Barna et al. 2016); J.L. Sánchez (ed.) (2019), *Espacios y prácticas económicas alternativas en las ciudades españolas*. Madrid: Thomson-Reuters Aranzadi; and the case studies on integrated area development and social innovation (Moulaert et al. 2010).
3. We write in 'spirit' because the Belgian federal government never ratified Article 31. This is an anomaly, because in this federal country housing is not under the national State's competencies; see Hubeau et al. 2021.

References

Andress, H.J. & Lohmann, H. (eds) (2008). *The Working Poor in Europe: Employment, Poverty and Globalisation*. Edward Elgar Publishing.

Barna, C., Irina, O. & Ancuța, V. (2016). Atlas of social economy 2014 edition: statistical overview of the reality of the social economy in Romania. *Revista de Economie Socială*, 6(1), 19–34.

Chandhoke, N. (2009). Putting civil society in its place. *Radical Politics Today*, 44(7), 6–7.

De Schutter, O. (2002). Europe in search of its civil society. *European Law Journal*, 8(2), 198–217.

De Schutter, O. & Dedeurwaerdere, T. (2021). *Social Innovation in the Service of Social and Ecological Transformation: The Rise of the Enabling State*. Routledge.

Demirovic, A. (ed.) (1992). *Hegemonie und Staat*. Westfälisches Dampfboot.

Eizaguirre, S., Pradel-Miquel, M. & García, M. (2017). Citizenship practices and democratic governance: 'Barcelona en Comú' as an urban citizenship confluence promoting a new policy agenda. *Citizenship Studies*, 21(4), 425–439.

Engelen, E., Froud, J., Johal, S., Salento, A. & Williams, K. (2017). The grounded city: from competitivity to the foundational economy. *Cambridge Journal of Regions, Economy and Society*, 10(3), 407–423.

García, M. & Moulaert, F. (2022). Governance in contemporary metropolises: quo vadis the state? In F. Tales (ed.), *Handbook on Local and Regional Governance*. Edward Elgar Publishing.

Hubeau, B., Dambre, M. & Bernard, N. (2021). Hoe oordeelt het Europees Comité voor Sociale Rechten over woonbeleid? Onderzoek naar het (Herzien) Europees Sociaal Handvest in een Vlaamse Context. Research report.

Jessop, B. (1995). The regulation approach, governance and post-Fordism: alternative perspectives on economic and political change? *Economy & Society*, 24(3), 307–333.

Jessop, B. (2006). Spatial Fixes, Temporal Fixes and Spatio-Temporal Fixes. In N. Castree and D. Gregory (eds), *David Harvey: A Critical Reader*, pp. 142–66, Blackwell Publishing.

Jessop, B. (2020). *Putting Civil Society in Its Place*. Policy Press.

Jessop, B. & Sum, N. (2019). Putting solidarity in its place in metagovernance. In P. van den Broeck, A. Mehmood, A. Paidakaki & C. Perra (eds), *Social Innovation as Political Transformation: Thoughts for a Better World*, 100–106. Edward Elgar Publishing.

Kelton, S. (2021). *The Deficit Spending Myth: How to Build a Better Economy*. John Murray.

Kenis, A. & Lievens, M. (2015). *The Limits of the Green Economy*. Routledge.

Le Monde diplomatique (2021). https://www.monde-diplomatique.fr/2021/07/DERENS/63318.

Lukács, G. (1972). *History and Class Consciousness: Studies in Marxist Dialectics*. MIT Press.

Mandel, E. (1972). *Der Spätkapitalismus: Versuch einer marxistischen Erklärung*. Suhrkamp Verlag.

Manganelli, A. & Moulaert, F. (2018). Hybrid governance tensions fuelling self-reflexivity in Alternative Food Networks: the case of the Brussels GASAP (solidarity purchasing groups for peasant agriculture). *Local Environment*, 23(8), 830–845.

Martinelli, F., Moulaert, F. & Novy, A. (2013). *Urban and Regional Development Trajectories in Contemporary Capitalism*. Routledge.

Moulaert, F. & Ailenei, O. (2005). Social economy, third sector and solidarity relations: a conceptual synthesis from history to present. *Urban Studies*, 42(11), 2037–2053.

Moulaert, F., Jessop, B. & Mehmood, A. (2016). Agency, structure, institutions, discourse (ASID) in urban and regional development. *International Journal of Urban Services*, 20(2), 167–187.

Moulaert, F. & MacCallum, D. (2019). *Advanced Introduction to Social Innovation.* Edward Elgar Publishing.

Moulaert, F. MacCallum, D., Van den Broeck, P. & Garcia, M. (2019). Bottom-linked governance and socially innovative political transformation. In J. Howaldt, C. Kaletka, A. Schröder & M. Zirngiebl (eds), *Atlas of Social Innovation. Second Volume: A World of New Practices*, 62–65. Signature Books.

Moulaert, F., & Nussbaumer, J. (2008). *Logique sociale du développement territorial.* PUQ.

Moulaert, F., Swyngedouw, E., Martinelli, F. & Gonzalez, S. (eds) (2010). *Can Neighbourhoods Save the City? Community Development and Social Innovation.* Routledge.

Paidakaki, A., Moulaert, F., Leinfelder, H. & Van den Broeck, P. (2020). Can pro-equity hybrid governance shape an egalitarian city? Lessons from post-Katrina New Orleans. *Territory, Politics, Governance*, 1–19. https://doi .org/10.1080/21622671.2020.1773919.

Polanyi, K. (2001 [1944]). *The Great Transformation: The Political and Economic Origins of Our Time.* Beacon Press.

Swyngedouw, E. (2021). Illiberalism and the democratic paradox: the infernal dialectic of neoliberal emancipation. *European Journal of Social Theory.* https:// doi.org/10.1177/13684310211027079.

Vicari Haddock, S. & Moulaert, F. (2009). *Rigenerare la città.* il Mulino.

White, R.J. (2009). Explaining why the non-commodified sphere of mutual aid is so pervasive in the advanced economies: some case study evidence from an English city. *International Journal of Sociology and Social Policy*, 29(9–10), 457–472.

Index

Printed and bound by CPI Group (UK) Ltd, Croydon, CR0 4YY

30/07/2023

03241317-0001